ADA: A Programmer's Conversion Course

THE ELLIS HORWOOD SERIES IN
COMPUTERS AND THEIR APPLICATIONS

Series Editor: BRIAN MEEK
Director of the Computer Unit, Queen Elizabeth College, University of London

The series aims to provide up-to-date and readable texts on the theory and practice of computing, with particular though not exclusive emphasis on computer applications. Preference is given in planning the series to new or developing areas, or to new approaches in established areas.

The books will usually be at the level of introductory or advanced undergraduate courses. In most cases they will be suitable as course texts, with their use in industrial and commercial fields always kept in mind. Together they will provide a valuable nucleus for a computing science library.

INTERACTIVE COMPUTER GRAPHICS IN SCIENCE TEACHING
Edited by J. McKENZIE, University College, London, L. ELTON, University of Surrey, R. LEWIS, Chelsea College, London.
INTRODUCTORY ALGOL 68 PROGRAMMING
D. F. BRAILSFORD and A. N. WALKER, University of Nottingham.
GUIDE TO GOOD PROGRAMMING PRACTICE
Edited by B. L. MEEK, Queen Elizabeth College, London and P. HEATH, Plymouth Polytechnic.
CLUSTER ANALYSIS ALGORITHMS: For Data Reduction and Classification of Objects
H. SPÄTH, Professor of Mathematics, Oldenburg University.
DYNAMIC REGRESSION: Theory and Algorithms
L. J. SLATER, Department of Applied Engineering, Cambridge University and
H. M. PESARAN, Trinity College, Cambridge
FOUNDATIONS OF PROGRAMMING WITH PASCAL
LAWRIE MOORE, Birkbeck College, London.
PROGRAMMING LANGUAGE STANDARDISATION
Edited by B. L. MEEK, Queen Elizabeth College, London and I. D. HILL, Clinical Research Centre, Harrow.
THE DARTMOUTH TIME SHARING SYSTEM
G. M. BULL, The Hatfield Polytechnic
RECURSIVE FUNCTIONS IN COMPUTER SCIENCE
R. PETER, formerly Eötvos Lorand University of Budapest.
FUNDAMENTALS OF COMPUTER LOGIC
D. HUTCHISON, University of Strathclyde.
THE MICROCHIP AS AN APPROPRIATE TECHNOLOGY
Dr. A. BURNS, The Computing Laboratory, Bradford University
SYSTEMS ANALYSIS AND DESIGN FOR COMPUTER APPLICATION
D. MILLINGTON, University of Strathclyde.
COMPUTING USING BASIC: An Interactive Approach
TONIA COPE, Oxford University Computing Teaching Centre.
RECURSIVE DESCENT COMPILING
A. J. T. DAVIE and R. MORRISON, University of St. Andrews, Scotland.
PROGRAMMING LANGUAGE TRANSLATION
R. E. BERRY, University of Lancaster
MICROCOMPUTERS IN EDUCATION
Edited by I. C. H. SMITH, Queen Elizabeth College, University of London
STRUCTURED PROGRAMMING WITH COMAL
R. ATHERTON, Bulmershe College of Higher Education
PASCAL IMPLEMENTATION: The P4 Compiler and Compiler and Assembler/Interpreter
S. PEMBERTON and M. DANIELS, Brighton Polytechnic
PRINCIPLES OF TEXT PROCESSING
F. N. TESKEY, University of Manchester
ADA: A PROGRAMMER'S CONVERSION COURSE
M. J. STRATFORD-COLLINS, U.S.A.
REAL TIME LANGUAGES
S. YOUNG, UMIST, Manchester
SOFTWARE ENGINEERING
K. GEWALD, G. HAAKE and W. PFADLER, Siemens AG, Munich

ADA: A Programmer's Conversion Course

M. J. STRATFORD-COLLINS, B.Sc.
Professional Computer Programmer
California, USA

ELLIS HORWOOD LIMITED
Publishers · Chichester

Halsted Press: a division of
JOHN WILEY & SONS
New York · Brisbane · Chichester · Toronto

First published in 1982 by
ELLIS HORWOOD LIMITED
Market Cross House, Cooper Street, Chichester, West Sussex, PO19 1EB, England

The publisher's colophon is reproduced from James Gillison's drawing of the ancient Market Cross, Chichester.

Distributors:

Australia, New Zealand, South-east Asia:
Jacaranda-Wiley Ltd., Jacaranda Press,
JOHN WILEY & SONS INC.,
G.P.O. Box 859, Brisbane, Queensland 40001, Australia

Canada:
JOHN WILEY & SONS CANADA LIMITED
22 Worcester Road, Rexdale, Ontario, Canada.

Europe, Africa:
JOHN WILEY & SONS LIMITED
Baffins Lane, Chichester, West Sussex, England.

North and South America and the rest of the world:
Halsted Press: a division of
JOHN WILEY & SONS
605 Third Avenue, New York, N.Y. 10016, U.S.A.

©1982 M. J. Stratford-Collins/Ellis Horwood Ltd.

British Library Cataloguing in Publication Data
Stratford-Collins, M. J.
ADA: a programmer's conversion course. —
(Ellis Horwood series in computers and their applications)
1. Ada (Computer program language)
I. Title
001.64.24   QA76.73.A35

Library of Congress Card No. 82-3042 AACR2

ISBN 0-85312-250-4 (Ellis Horwood Limited, Publishers — Library Edition)
ISBN 0-85312-444-2 (Ellis Horwood Limited, Publishers — Student Edition)
ISBN 0-470-27332-1 (Halsted Press)

Typeset in Press Roman by Ellis Horwood Ltd.
Printed in Great Britain by R. J. Acford, Chichester.

Table of Contents

Author's Preface

The Ada programming language is the culmination of an intense work effort. It was initiated by the United States Department of Defense High Order Language Working Group (HOLWG) in 1975, with the aim of providing a single programming language for all of their embedded systems.

This book is aimed at providing the professional programmer with an easy means to learn the basics of Ada. It therefore assumes that the reader has knowledge of at least one other high level programming language (preferably a block-structured one such as Pascal). It is not intended to be a primer on programming, nor a reference manual for every nook and cranny of the language. It concentrates instead on those features which will be used most often, by most programmers.

The first five chapters are designed to cover the basic language elements which are common to most modern procedural languages. Chapter 1 is an introduction, Chapter 2 is concerned with control over program flow, Chapters 3 and 4 with data types and data structures and Chapter 5 with procedures and functions. Chapters 6, 7, 8 and 9 cover the package concept, the generic concept, support for exception handling and language constructs for tasking support, respectively. Chapter 10 is devoted to a discussion of the issues of program structure, and name scope and visibility, and the book closes with a chapter covering the Input and Output facilities provided by Ada. For reference purposes, Appendix A provides a syntax definition of the language (in alphabetical order) while Appendix B contains a list of Ada's reserved words.

I would like to take this opportunity to thank all of my family and friends who have encouraged and guided me as the manuscript was taking shape. I am particularly indebted to my wife, without whose unfailing support this work would not have been possible.

For Janet

CHAPTER 1

Basics

The purpose of all except the most trivial programs, written in any language, is to manipulate data. It is thus of paramount importance that the computer be informed how the various different data objects which it will encounter are represented. The material covered in this chapter will provide the reader with a knowledge of the basic elements (identifiers, simple data types, literals, and constants) which are manipulated by an ada program. The concluding paragraphs will introduce the concepts of "scope" and "visibility" and their relation to program structure.

1.1 GETTING STARTED

We shall start by analysing a simple program fragment, whose purpose is to read (from some generalised input device) a number which represents a temperature on the Fahrenheit scale, convert it to the Celsius scale, and write out the result of the conversion (to a generalised output device).

```
1     declare
2          Celsius, Fahrenheit  :  float;
3     begin
4          get(Fahrenheit);
5          Celsius := (Fahrenheit-32)*5/9;
6          put(Celsius);
7     end;  - - of program fragment
```

The first line, the 'declare', marks the start of this program segment, or block. Its purpose is to inform the compiler that declarations of any variables to be used in the block will now follow. The third line, the 'begin', marks the start of any executable statements, and it is matched by a terminating 'end' on line 7. The begin-end can be thought of as a pair of brackets, enclosing a series of statements.

Line 2 contains the "declaration" statement. Its function is to create variables named "Celsius" and "Fahrenheit", neither of whose values are currently known. Included in the declaration of each variable is its "type". The concept of type is common to many modern languages (e.g. Algol and Pascal) and is one of the most important features of Ada. Among other things, it allows the compiler to check that the programmer is not trying to assign a value, an 'integer' number for example, to a variable of different type, 'character' perhaps.

Lines 4, 5 and 6 are the lines which perform the actual calculation. Line 4 will invoke a system utility called 'get', which will read a value into the variable Fahrenheit. Having read a value into Fahrenheit, we must convert it to a number on the Celsius scale, according to some formula, and place the result into the variable named Celsius. This is performed by the single 'assignment' statement on line 5. This statement will evaluate the expression on the right-hand side of the assignment symbol (the ":=") and "assign" that value to the variable on the left-hand side, in this case Celsius. The new value will overwrite any value which had previously been stored there.

All that now remains to be done is to print the value in Celsius, as in Line 6. Line 7 marks the end of the segment which was started by the 'declare' on line 1. Note that it also contains a comment. A comment string is started by the character pair "--" and is terminated by the end of the line. Comments are ignored by the compiler.

There is one point about the example which bears repetition, since it is of fundamental importance. Ada demands that the programmer define *EVERY* variable or constant which will be used by means of declaration statements. The information required is the name, or more correctly the 'identifier', and the 'type', which specifies to the compiler how this new data object is to be represented. Ada does not support or allow default declarations, as there are in Fortran for example. By forcing the programmer to define all of the attributes of his variables and constants before they are used, some of the potential for making mistake is eliminated, whilst at the same time allowing greater scope for compile-time and run-time checks to be made.

1.2 CONSTANTS

In lines 2 and 3 we created variables which could have data read from them or written to them. In some programs, we may wish to define a data object whose value we know and which will in all probability never need to be changed. We would like, however, to make it easy to change at some later date, if it proves necessary. An example of this might be in a stock control program which automatically prints a re-order form for some more elephants when stocks fall below 10 pieces. We might, in the program, define a constant as follows:

reorder_elephants : **constant** *integer* := 10;

and thereafter refer to the re-order quantity as *"reorder_elephants"*. If, at some time in the future, we wish to keep at least 15 on hand, then we have only to change one item, the value of the constant as specified in its declaration, and recompile the program. Compare this to the task of scanning several thousand lines of the program text for the digits "10", determining whether they refer to the re-order quantity for elephants and then changing them to "15", and you will see the benefit of using constants. Note that variables and constants differ in one major respect, in that constants may never be written to once they have been defined (they may never appear on the left of an assignment symbol). This again eliminates a possible source of error, since a statement like:

reorder_elephants := first_of_month;

written where ther programmer intended to write:

reorder_elephants_date := first_of_month;

would cause the compiler to flag the statement as an error, since by definition constants cannot have their value altered.

In spite of all that we have said about the benefits of using constants, there are still circumstances when we know, absolutely and categorically, that a value is never going to change. There will always be 1000 metres in a kilometer, and the conversion factors in the original Fahrenheit to Celsius example will always remain the same. There is, therefore, no particular advantage to declaring them as constants, when we could just as well write them directly into our program where they are used, sure in the knowledge that we will never need to alter them. A value used in this way is called a 'literal' value, examples of which are the "32", "5" and "9" in our sample. As we discuss the various data types in the following sections, we will see in more detail how literals of each type may be used.

1.3 CHARACTER SETS

The character set available with a particular Ada compiler is implementation dependent, although the language definition requires that all implementations provide, at a minimum, the following:

```
        A  B  C  ..  X  Y  Z
        0  1  2  ..  7  8  9
"  #  &  '  ( )  *  + ,  − . / : ; < = > _ |
              the space character
```

We shall assume throughout this book, that the rest of the ASCII character set is also provided, adding:

```
        a  b  c  ..  x  y  z
    !  $  %  ?  @  [ \ ]  ^ ` { }  ~
```

to our repertoire. Finally, we shall assume that the character set is ordered such that:

$$0 < 1 \, . \, . < 9 < A < B \, . \, . < Z < a \, . \, . < z$$

While the ordering given here is one of the most common, there are systems in existence which are different. If you are in any doubt, refer to the implementation guide for your site's compiler for details of the sequence used. Similarly, if you are in doubt about the character set available at your site, refer to the compiler documentation (in the package called STANDARD).

1.4 IDENTIFIERS

An identifier is a sequence of characters used to denote a declared program element (e.g. a constant, variable, subprogram, etc.). The rules for the generation of identifiers are as follows:

(a) an identifier must start with a letter.
(b) subsequent characters may be letters, decimal digits or the underscore character.
(c) an identifier may be composed of any number of characters.
(d) if lower case letters are used, then no distinction is made between upper and lower case instances of the same letter.

A convenient form of shorthand for stating these rules is a variant of the Backus-Naur Form, as shown below:

> *identifier* ::= *letter* { [*underscore*] *letter_or_digit* }
> *letter_or_digit* ::= *letter* | *digit*
> *letter* ::= *upper_case_letter* | *lower_case_letter*

Lower case words (possibly including underscore characters) denote a syntactic category, as for example upper_case_letter. The braces, { }, signify that the enclosed part may be repeated any number of times, including zero. Square brackets, [ ], denote that the entity enclosed within is optional. The following examples serve to illustrate the rules.

today	– – valid
tomorrow	– – also valid
next_thursday	– – valid again
todays%	– – invalid, '%' is not a letter, digit or '_'
week51	– – valid
4_next_week	– – invalid, does not start with a letter
next-week	– – invalid, '-' is not a letter, digit or '_'

There are two pieces of information about identifiers which are not contained in the definition, but which are nevertheless of the utmost importance.

They should be well understood, as they may otherwise lead to some confusion. Firstly, as a consequence of upper and lower case letters being treated identically by the compiler when it is checking identifiers, PI, Pi, pi and pI would all be determined to be the same identifier and would thus all refer to the same data object. Secondly, the Ada compiler will inspect *every* character in an identifier when checking to see whether two identifiers are the same, unlike compilers for some languages, which will only check the first six, eight, etc.

There are certain words in the Ada language which have the form of identifiers and conform to the rules by which identifiers are generated, but which are "reserved" for use by the compiler. Some examples, which have already been met in the original program fragment, are **'begin'**, **'end'**, **'declare'**. Because of their special syntactic role, these words may not be used by the programmer as identifiers. In all examples, reserved words are printed in **heavy** type to distinguish them from identifiers. For reference purposes, a complete list of reserved words appears in Appendix B.

1.5 SIMPLE DATA TYPES

In order to manipulate a data object correctly, a program has to know how that data object is represented on the machine on which the program will run, how to access it, what is the legal range of values for the object, and what operations can be performed on it. Each 'type' in Ada has an associated set of attributes which uniquely define an object of that type. Examples of attributes are the precision with which a real number is to be stored, a range specification defining a legal range of values or the length of an array. The two strings 'us' and 'them' can be considered to be of the same type, string, but with different length attributes, 2 and 4. Note that all objects of the same type have the same set of attributes but that individual objects may have different values of a particular attribute. The purpose of the declaration statement is to convey this information to the compiler.

At this point, having introduced the concept of 'type', it will be instructive to see how it is used to generate objects. This is done with an 'object declaration', whose purpose is to generate an object of the given type, and hence with a given set of attributes, give values to those attributes and to associate the newly created object with the identifier supplied by the programmer. This is called the 'elaboration' of the declaration (Note: In order to be consistent with the terminology used in the Ada Reference Manual, we shall use the convention that declarations are 'elaborated', expressions are 'evaluated', and statements are 'executed'). Some examples of declarations are:

```
period      : constant character := '.';
I_ten       : integer := 10;
R_ten       : float    := 10;
count       : integer;
```

Ada programs may be required to represent many differing entities depending on the particular application. Thus, for example, for a scientific problem we may need to represent vectors, while in a project control program we might want to represent available resources. As an aid to the programmer, Ada provides a built-in set of representations for the more commonly encountered entities, or 'types', as well as allowing us to generate our own more sophisticated types which can better represent the data with which we have to work. It is this ability to create user-oriented types which is one of the most powerful features of Ada. In this chapter we shall cover the predefined types 'boolean', 'character', 'integer', 'float' and 'fixed'. Discussion of the types which are generated from these five and the user-definable types will be convered later.

1.6 ENUMERATION TYPES

There are certain classes of objects which can take only discrete values, examples being variables which represent the days of the week (Monday, Tuesday, etc.), the months of the year (January, February, etc.), the gender of a person (male, female) etc. In order for the compiler to know what values are valid for such an object and what their ordering is to be, the values must be 'enumerated' when the type is defined (refer to Chatper 3 for details of type declaration). A type which requires this sort of definition is called an 'enumeration type', and the Ada language has built-in definitions for the boolean and character enumeration types.

1.6.1 Boolean Type

A boolean data object is used to represent the logical truth values true and false, which are the only values an object of this type may take. In Ada it provides the same sort of capabilities as the Fortran LOGICAL and the Algol or Pascal boolean types. Only two literals are associated with the boolean type: 'true' and 'false', ordered such that $false < true$. The predefined operators for boolean objects are:

and   **or**   **xor**   =   /=

each of which operates between a pair of operands (they are 'dyadic' operators) and the operator:

not

which operates on a single operand (it is a 'monadic' operator). The following truth tables define the results of using these operators for various values of the operands (f=false, t=true):

p	not$p$
f	t
t	f

p	q	$p$and$q$	$p$or$q$	$p$xor$q$	p=q	p/=q
f	f	f	f	f	t	f
f	t	f	t	t	f	t
t	f	f	t	t	f	t
t	t	t	t	f	t	f

Note that in the above tables, p and q need not be declared boolean objects. They may be expressions, so long as they evaluate to yield a boolean result. Thus, we could write:

> **if** ($qty\_on\_hand < min\_qty$) **or** $special\_case$ **then** . . . **endif**;

The term in the brackets evaluates to a boolean result and so it is legal to use it with the **or** operator. A typical use of a boolean variable might be to control the flow of control of a program, as given below:

> end_of_file : $boolean := false$; -- declaration of the object
> **if** end_of_file **then** . . . **endif**; -- use of the object

An enumeration type is a member of the set of discrete types, made up as the name suggests, of those types which can only take discrete values. There are five attribute enquiry functions associated with discrete types which allow the programmer to determine the range and ordering of the permissible values (although the results are not particularly interesting for this type):

> $boolean'first$ -- minimum value of permitted range
>   (false)
> $boolean'last$ -- maximum value of permitted range
>   (true)
> $boolean'succ(false)$ -- next value in sequence
> $boolean'pred(true)$ -- previous value in sequence
> $boolean'pos(x)$ -- position of x within legal range of a boolean
>   object (0 for $false$ and 1 for $true$).

If an attempt is made to ask for the successor to true or the predecessor of false, then the RANGE_ERROR exception will be generated.

The other two enquiry functions ($'first$ and $'last$) are applicable to any scalar type ($boolean$, $character$, $integer$, $float$, $fixed$ and any of the enumeration types).

1.6.2 Character Type

There are many applications which require that a program be able to manipulate character data (e.g. compilers, word-processors, etc.). Unlike many of the older languages such as Fortran-IV or Algol-60, Ada provides the built-in type character for the purpose of representing single characters. Like the boolean type, this is an enumeration type, except that in this case there is a more meaningful range. To illustrate, the type declaration for the character type is:

```
type character is
(NUL,    SOH,    STX,    ETX,    EOT,    ENQ,    ACK,    BEL,
 BS,     HT,     LF,     VT,     FF,     CR,     SO,     SI,
 DLE,    DC1,    DC2,    DC3,    DC4,    NAK,    SYN,    ETB,
 CAN,    EM,     SUB,    ESC,    FS,     GS,     RS,     US,
 ' ',    '!',    '"',    '#',    '$',    '%',    '&',    ''',
 '(',    ')',    '*',    '+',    ',',    '-',    '.',    '/',
 '0',    '1',    '2',    '3',    '4',    '5',    '6',    '7',
 '8',    '9',    ':',    ';',    '<',    '=',    '>',    '?',
 '@',    'A',    'B',    'C',    'D',    'E',    'F',    'G',
 'H',    'I',    'J',    'K',    'L',    'M',    'N',    'O',
 'P',    'Q',    'R',    'S',    'T',    'U',    'V',    'W',
 'X',    'Y',    'Z',    '[',    '\',    ']',    '^',    '_',
 '`',    'a',    'b',    'c',    'd',    'e',    'f',    'g',
 'h',    'i',    'j',    'k',    'l',    'm',    'n',    'o',
 'p',    'q',    'r',    's',    't',    'u',    'v',    'w',
 'x',    'y',    'z',    '{',    '|',    '}',    '~',    DEL);
```

Note that the names of the ASCII control characters are used here only for clarity; they are not identifiers and should not be used as such.

The ordering of an enumeration type such as this is exactly that which is specified in the enumeration. Thus, for the character type, 'A' is less than 'B' which is less than 'C' etc., giving the collating sequence (for those readers who are familiar with Cobol or other languages).

The same five attribute enquiry functions are available for character variables as were available for boolean variables. The following examples serve to illustrate their usage:

character'first   -- NUL
character'last   -- DEL
character'pred('A') -- '@'
character'succ('A') -- 'B'
character'pos(BEL) -- 7 (note that the value of the function
                             character'pos (*character'first*) is 0)

We can now see how an attribute enquiry function might be used to determine whether the lower case alphabet is supported:

if *character'last* < *lower_case*_A **then** ... **endif**;

1.7 NUMBERS

In order to perform numerical calculations on a computer, we need to be able to represent numbers. There are two different representations for numbers in Ada, exact (integer) and approximate (float and fixed). This distinction is drawn since it is possible to represent exactly any integer number (given a sufficiently large number of bits) whereas real numbers can only be approximated to a given degree of accuracy (how, for instance, do you represent the fraction '1/3' with a finite number of bits?). The next three sections deal with the simple types associated with numeric representations.

1.7.1 Integer

Numbers from the set of integers (whole numbers such as 25, 1024, 0 and −3) are represented by objects of the type integer. As noted above, given the right number of bits we could represent any integer number. This is not practical, however, so Ada provides the attribute enquiry functions *integer'first* and *integer'last* to enable the programmer to determine what range of values can be represented by the type integer. Thus, for example, on a machine which uses a twos complement, 16-bit representation for integers,

$$integer'first = -32768 \quad \text{-- the smallest integer}$$
$$integer'last = 32767 \quad \text{-- the largest integer}$$

It is important to note that an the exception CONSTRAINT_ERROR will be raised if an attempt is made to assign a value to an object whose type cannot represent a value that large (or small), as shown below:

```
a, b, c : integer;   -- 2s complement, 16-bit assumed

a := 10_000;
b := 10_000;
c := a * b;          -- CONSTRAINT_ERROR raised here
```

The usual operators are defined for this type, both operands and results being of type integer. They are:

$x**y$	-- exponentiation
$x*y$	-- multiplication
x/y	-- integer division
$x\,rem\,y$	-- remaindering
$x\,mod\,y$	-- modulus
$x+y$	-- addition
$x-y$	-- subtraction
$+x$	-- unary plus
$-x$	-- unary minus

and the operator hierarchy, in descending order of precedence is:

$$* \quad / \quad \textbf{rem} \quad \overset{**}{\textbf{mod}}$$
$$+ \quad - \quad\quad -- \text{ unary}$$
$$+ \quad - \quad\quad -- \text{ adding}$$

We can combine these operators with integer literals, constants and variables to form integer expressions such as:

weeks * 7
years * 52 + *days*
feet * 12
length * *breadth*

and we can use these expressions in tests and in assignment statements. With the following declarations:

area, length, breadth : *integer*;
hours, days, overtime, vacation : *integer*;

we could write statements of the form:

area := *length* * *breadth*;

or

hours := *days* * 8 + *overtime*;
if *hours*+*vaction* > *max_time* **then** . . . **endif**;

The integer type provides for numbers which are useful not only in calculations, but also where the programmer requires counters and indices:

for *count* **in** 1 . . 5 **loop**
    put (*zip_code(count)*);
end loop;

while $x < 10$ **loop**
    put $(x*x)$;
    $x := x + 1$;
end loop;

Some further explanation of the operator for integer division, /, is required. With all of the above operators, the result is of the same type (integer) as the operands. Thus, the expression '4/5' will yield an integer result whose value is zero, whilst the expression '5/5' will yield a result whose value is one. This is an easy trap for the unwary programmer to fall into, especially when using a language such as Ada, where the symbols for the integer and real division operators are the same, in contrast to languages such as Algol-60 and Algol-68 where they were deliberately chosen to be different. It can, however, be used to advantage as in the next example, which calculates the time difference between Greenwich and a given longitude:

declare
        longitude, time_difference : *integer*;
                     direction : *character*;
begin
        get(*longitude*);   -- in degrees, 0-180
        get(*direction*);   -- 'W'=west, 'E'=east
        time_difference := *longitude*/15; -- integer division!
        if *direction* = 'W' **then**
          time_difference := −*time_difference*;
        endif;
        put(*longitude*);
        put(*direction*);
        put(*time_difference*);
end;

1.7.2 Float

The float and fixed types allow us to represent real numbers approximately on a computer, the difference between the two being in how the approximation is handled. It is the equivalent of the REAL type in languages such as Fortran. The float type places a relative bound on the error in the representation by specifying the accuracy with which objects are to be held. The accuracy is defined in terms of the number of decimal digits required for the mantissa when the number is represented as shown below:

    .dddddddEee -- digits = 6

The Ada language specifies that both the range of representable numbers and the accuracy with which they are kept is dependent upon the particular implementation. They may be determined using the attribute enquiry functions:

    float'**digits** -- number of decimal digits accuracy
                    (an integer object)
    float'*small* -- smallest positive value representable
    float'*large* -- largest positive value representable

Since the accuracy is defined in terms of the length of the mantissa, for convenience the function

    float'*epsilon*

is provided, to allow the programmer to determine the 'granularity' of the representation. It is the absolute value of the difference between 1.0 and the next number above 1.0. Note that it is distinct from *float'small*, because *float'small* is dependent on the size of both the mantissa and the exponent.

The operators which are defined for objects of type float are:

$$+ \quad - \quad * \quad /$$

each returning a result of type float, and the exponentiation operator

$$**$$

which is used to raise a float object to an integer power, the result again being of type float. Note that in Ada it is illegal to attempt to raise a number to a non-integer power. The examples which follow serve to illustrate the use of float variables:

```
declare
    height, time_to_fall : float;
                        g : constant float := 32; -- fps/s
begin
    get(height);
    time_to_fall := sqrt(2*height/g); -- sqrt = square-root
    put(time_to_fall);
end;
```

```
declare
    radius, area, circumference : float;
    pi : constant float := 3.14159;
begin
    get(radius);
    area := pi * radius * radius;
    circumference := 2 * pi * radius;
    put(area);
    put(circumference);
end;
```

Note that we could have calculated the area using the following statement:

```
area := pi * radius**2;
```

with exactly the same results.

Ada is a strongly typed language, which means that the programmer is forbidden to mix objects of differing types within an expression or assignment. All of the examples so far encountered have been contrived to skirt the problem. This is an unreasonable restriction to place on any programmer who is working in the real world, since it is extremely common to have to perform calculations which require operands or parameters of differing types. The mechanism in Ada

which allows these calculations is 'type conversion', which will convert an
expression from one type to another, provided the conversion is legal. Note that
unlike Algol or Pascal, Ada requires that all type conversions be written
explicitly, thus serving the dual purposes of highlighting the places where
a conversion is necessary, and removing the possibility that the compiler will do
something the programmer did not intend. Here are some examples of type
conversion:

```
declare
     gross_pay  :  float;
     hourly_pay  :  constant float := 3.12;
     empl_no, no_of_empl, hours, I  :  integer;
begin
     get(no_of_empl);
     for i in 1.. no_of_empl loop
         get(empl_no);
         get(hours);
         gross_pay := hourly_pay * float(hours);
         put(empl_no);
         put(gross_pay);
     end loop;
end;
```

In general, conversion of an object's value from one type to another is achieved
by writing:

```
target_type(expression)
```

which delivers the result of the expression as an object of the *target_type*. Note
that type conversions are only allowed between closely related types.

```
declare
     degrees  :  integer;
     radians  :  float;
          pi  :  constant float := 3.14159;
begin
     get(degrees);
     radians := pi/180*float(degrees);
     put(radians);
end;
```

1.7.3 Fixed
In addition to the float type, real numbers can be approximately represented by
an object of the fixed type. In this case, however, an absolute bound is placed

on the error as opposed to the relative bound of the float type. In some applications on small computers, fixed point representation of real numbers has an advantage in that numerical calculations can be performed at a speed which floating point calculations cannot match without the addition of (expensive) hardware.

The same operators apply to objects of type fixed as to objects of type float, and the attribute enquiry function

fixed'delta

returns the 'granularity' of the type, as specified when the type was defined (see Chatper 3). The enquiry function

fixed'actual_delta

returns the implemented value of delta. The value of the delta of the fixed type is implementation dependent. It may be found either by using the enquiry function or by looking in the package called STANDARD, which is supplied with every implementation.

1.8 INTRODUCTION TO SCOPE

In the examples which we have met so far, we have 'delcared' all of the identifiers we wanted to use before their use, as Ada requires. No mention has been given, however, to the range of text over which a particular identifier is accessible (i.e. when is an identifier 'visible' and when is it not?). The problem is best illustrated by the following:

```
A : declare                      -- start of outer block (A)
        alpha, beta : character;
    begin
        get(alpha);              --- get a character
        B : declare              -- start of inner block (B)
            alpha : integer;
            begin
            get(alpha);          -- get an integer
            put(alpha);          -- put an integer
            end B;
        put(alpha);              -- put a character
    end A;
```

If we write to alpha in B, which object does the identifier refer to? The answer lies in the 'block structure' and the 'visibility rules'. The block labelled 'B' is said to be enclosed in the outer block, 'A' and hence all declarations in 'A' are visible in 'B', unless there is a clash, in which case the innermost declaration is the visible one (unless we take special action). The reverse is not true. None of the objects declared in 'B' are visible in 'A'. To override the 'hiding' in the previous example, we would have to write:

```
A : declare
        alpha : character;
    begin
        get(alpha);
        B : declare
                alpha : integer;
            begin
                get(alpha);        -- the integer
                put(alpha);        -- the integer
                put(A.alpha);      -- the character
            end B;
        put(alpha);                -- the character
        put(B.alpha);              -- illegal, the integer
                                   -- no longer exists.
    end A;
```

The rules for scope and visibility are complex, and this section serves only as an introduction. The subject is covered in detail later.

CHAPTER 2

Flow of Control

In this chapter, we shall investigate the basic control structures available to the Ada programmer; **loop, while, for, exit, if, case, goto** and **raise**. These are used to change the sequence of statement execution from the normal line-by-line pattern.

2.1 THE LOOP STATEMENTS

The **loop** statement causes a series of statements to be repeatedly executed until a specified condition is met. The syntactical definition for the **loop** is:

loop_statement ::=
    [*loop_identifier*:] [*iteration_clause*] *basic_loop*
    [*loop_identifier*] ;

basic_loop ::=
    loop
        sequence_of_statements
    end loop

iteration_clause ::=
    for *loop_parameter* **in** [**reverse**] *discrete_range*
  | **while** *condition*

loop_parameter ::= *identifier*

A brief study of the definitions will show that we can build several different styles of loop, choosing the one which is best suited to a given application. There is the basic loop for endless execution of the same sequence of statements, the **for** loop for execution of the loop body a specified number of times, and the **while** loop for repeated execution of the body until a given condition is met.

Before we examine the various loops in detail, there is one further point regarding the syntax definition which needs to be clarified. Although the definition shows that the trailing *loop_identifier* is optional, it is *required* if the initial *loop_identifier* is specified. In other words, if a loop has been given a *loop_identifier* at the beginning, then omission of the matching one at the end will cause a compilation error.

2.1.1 The Basic Loop

A basic loop will result in an infinite execution of the body of the loop, as in the following example:

```
automatic_teller:
    loop
        get_next_transaction(transaction_type);
        case transaction_type is
            when withdrawal => subtract;
            when    deposit =>     add;
            when   transfer => shuffle;
            when    balance => compute;
            when     others =>    null;
        end case;
    end loop automatic_teller;
```

The important feature of this type of loop is that it has no iteration clause. Thus, once the loop has been entered, there is no way out, and the sequence of statements which constitute the body of the loop will be executed for ever (this is not strictly true, however, because we can include an **exit** or **raise** statement in the loop body, as we shall see later in the chapter).

2.1.2 The While Loop

Now that we have been introduced to the basic loop, let use see what happens when it is modified by the inclusion of an iteration clause, producing a **while** loop:

```
find_last_item:
    while list_entry(i) /= last loop
        i := i + 1;
    end loop find_last_item;
    next;
```

The basic loop now includes an interation clause at the top, the effect of which is to cause the condition specified in the **while** clause to be evaluated before every execution of the loop body. If the condition evaluates to the boolean value *'true'* then the statements which make up the body of the loop will be executed and the condition re-evaluated. This sequence of "*test. . . execute, test. . . execute,* etc." will continue for as long as the condition evaluates to *'true'*. On the first occasion that it evaluates to *false,* however, the loop is abandoned and execution continues with the statement which follows the end of the loop, "*next;*" in the example.

The **while** loop provides us with a more powerful tool than the basic loop, since we can now specify a loop termination condition, as in the next examples, taken from a control system application and a simple search:

```
        read(actual_position);
    valve_position:
        while abs(desired_position − actual_position) > deadband
        loop
            error := desired_position − actual_position;
            correction := correction_calc (error);
            output_signal (correction);
            delay 5.0;
            read (actual_position);
        end loop valve_position;

        i := 1;
    find_me:
        while my_rec(i).name /= my_name and i <= imax loop
            i := i + 1;
        end loop find_me;
```

It is important to note that the inclusion of an iteration clause does not guarantee that the loop will ever terminate. The potential for programming an infinite loop is still present, as can be readily demonstrated:

```
state := true;              −− initialise Boolean variable
while state = true loop     −− always true
    null;                   −− do nothing
end loop;
next;                       −− will never be executed
```

In summary, a **while** loop will only terminate if the condition initially evaluates to *'false'* or if the outcome of the condition is in some way dependent upon the execution of the body, such that a *'false'* outcome will eventually be obtained.

2.1.3 The For Loop

The last member of the **loop** family is the **for** loop. In this type of loop, the iteration clause specifies a set of discrete values which are to be successively assigned to a *loop_parameter,* one per iteration:

```
for i in 1 . . 10 loop
    put (i * i);
end loop;
```

The effect of this is to set "i" to 1, test for $i \leq 10$ and if the result is $'true'$, print the value of i^2. This sequence is repeated, except that the next value in the range 1. .10 is assigned each time, until the test for $i \leq 10$ evaluates to $'false'$, which results in the printing of:

     1 4 9 16 25 36 49 64 81 100

There is no requirement in Ada that the range start at 1, nor that the range be limited to positive numbers. Thus, we could write:

    for i **in** $-20.$ $.-15$ **loop**
        put $(i * i)$;
    end loop;

which would print the sequence:

     400 361 324 289 256 225

Now, consider:

    for i **in** *young* . . *old* **loop**
        premium $(i) := i * factor(i) + base\_rate$;
    end loop;

In this example, the range of values over which the loop is to iterate has been specified using variables instead of literals. This is especially useful where either or both end points of the range are calculated values, since the **for** loop now handles the case of the null range without requiring any explicit testing on the part of the programmer (a range is said to be a null range when the lower bound exceeds the upper bound, i.e. *young* > *old*). A final word in connection with ranges: the range of a **for** loop is only calculated once, on entry into the loop, so it cannot be modified from within the body of the loop.

    The *loop_parameter*, $'i'$ is considered to be a variable local to the loop in its scope (i.e. it $'exists'$ only within the loop) and its value cannot be altered from within the body of the loop. It cannot, therefore, appear on the left-hand side of an assignment statement, nor as a modifiable (**out** or **inout**) parameter to a procedure call. The type of the *loop_parameter* is derived from the type of the loop's range, and thus a **for** loop can be used to step through a range of integer's, character's or any of the enumeration types, even user defined ones.

    It is often desirable to be able to step through a range in reverse order, from 10. .1 for example, instead of from 1. .10. If we were to write:

    for i **in** 10. .1 **loop**
        put $(i * i)$;
    end loop;

the loop would never be executed because the initial value of i would be greater than the final value, which is the definition of a null range. There exists, therefore, a reserved word **reverse** which causes a loop to be executed with successive values of the *loop_parameter* being in descending order instead of the normal ascending order. Thus:

```
for i in reverse 1..10 loop
    put (i * );
end loop;
```

results in the sequence

100 81 64 49 36 25 16 9 4 1

Some illustrative examples of loops are:

```
work_hours:
    for i in monday.. friday loop
        total_hours := total_hours + daily_hours(i);
    end loop work_hours;
```

```
countdown:                        -- "ten. . .nine. . .eight. . ."
    for i in reverse 0..10 loop
        speak_int(i);
        delay 1.0;
    end loop countdown;
```

```
scan_again:
    while refs_satisfied_this_pass > 0 loop
        rescan(library_list);
    end loop scan_again;
```

2.2 THE EXIT STATEMENT

The basic loop is, on its own, rather restrictive, and the **for** and **while** loops make their tests only at the top of the loop. What is needed is a generalised form of looping and testing. Ada provides this by combining the **exit** statement with the previous loop constructs:

```
exit_statement ::=
    exit [loop_name] [when condition] ;
```

The purpose of the **exit** is twofold. Firstly, it gives the programmer the freedom to place one or more tests for loop termination conditions anywhere within the body of the loop, and secondly, it explicitly marks the point(s) of departure from the loop. This greatly improves the readability and coding of certain loops.

```
get (my_record);
xfer:
    while my_record /= end_of_file loop
        put (my_record);
        get (my_record);
    end loop xfer;
```

The main point to note here is the initial *"get"* is only required because of the deficiencies inherent in applying a **while** construct to this particular case; it is not part of the original problem. Now let's see how the same problem may be recorded with a basic loop and an **exit**:

> *xfer*:
>> **loop**
>>> *get* (*my_record*);
>>> **exit** *xfer* **when** *my_record* = *end_of_file*;
>>> *put* (*my_record*);
>> **end loop** *xfer*;

With this structure, there are no superfluous statements, it is just as readable as the **while** version and more readable than an **if. . .goto** combination. Note that the loop is terminated only if the **when** clause evaluates to *'true'*.

The **exit** may optionally specify a *loop_name*. If the name is omitted, the loop in which the **exit** statement lexically resides will be left. If the name is supplied then the **exit** will be to the end of the enclosing named loop. It is illegal to use an **exit** statement to jump from an outer loop to an inner one, or to jump out of a procedure or a package.

2.3 THE IF STATEMENT

The **if** statement is used to choose a sequence of statements to be executed from a set of such sequences, dependent upon the logical outcome of one or more conditions.

> *if_statement* ::=
>> **if** *condition* **then**
>>> *sequence_of_statements*
>> { **elsif** *condition* **then**
>>> *sequence_of_statements* }
>> [**else**
>>> *sequence_of_statements*]
>> **end if**;

A brief study of the above syntax definition will show that we can generate statements with any of the following forms:

> if. . .then. . .end if;
> if. . .then. . .else. . .end if;
> if. . .then. . .elsif. . .then. . .end if;
> if. . .then. . .elsif. . .then. . .else. . .end if;

Note that the syntax of the **if** statement in Ada solves the "dangling else" problem inherent in Algol-60 and its derivatives, such as Pascal. An illustration of the problem is given in the example below (which would by syntactically illegal in Ada):

> **if** *a* **then if** *b* **then** *put*("*B*") **else** *put*("*C*");

Since the termination of both **if** statements is implied by the final semicolon, the example can be interpreted in either of two ways:

> **if** *a* **then**
>   **if** *b* **then** *put*("*B*")
>   **else** *put*("*C*");   -- requires *a* = true to print '*C*'

or

> **if** *a* **then**
>   **if** *b* **then** *put*("*B*")
>   **else** *put*("*C*");   -- requires *a* = false to print '*C*'

The decision to solve this problem in the syntax of Ada seems to be preferable to the limiting approach in Pascal and the implied solution with the block-IF of Fortran 77.

As may be seen from the above, the **if** statement, when executed, evaluates the condition, and if the result is '*true*' then the sequence of statements following the **then** is executed. After the last statement of this sequence is executed, the next statement to be executed will be the one following the **end if** statement.

If the initial condition evaluates to '*false*', then control passes to an **elisf** or **else** clause, and the corresponding statements are executed. After the last of these statements has been executed, we go to the statement following the **end if**, as before.

Some legal examples of Ada **if** statements are:

> **if** *deposits* < *withdrawals* **then**
>   *put*("*You are overdrawn*");
> **end if**;

> **if** *aircraft. trajectory* = *inbound* **then**
>   **if** *aircraft. id* /= *ours* **then**
>   *launch_interceptors*;
>   **else**
>   *notify_operator*;
>   **end if**;
>
> **end if**;

> **if** *trip_length* <= *short* **then**
>   *pack*(*toothbrush*);
> **elsif** *trip_length* <= *medium* **then**
>   *pack*(*small_bag*);
> **else**
>   *pack*(*trunk*);
> **end if**;

2.4 THE CASE STATEMENT

The **case** statement is used to pick a sequence of statements to be executed from a set of mutually exclusive choices, based on the value of an expression:

case_statement ::=
    case *expression* **is**
        { **when** *choice* { | *choice* } => *sequence_of_statements* }
    end case;

choice ::= *simple_expression* | *discrete_range* | **others**

Its function is analogous to the Algol-60 SWITCH, the Fortran Computed–GOTO, and the Pascal or Algol-68 CASE. The given expression (which must yield a value from one of the discrete types) is evaluated and the result is tested for a match with one of the choices. If a match is found, then the corresponding sequence of statements is executed, and control then passes to the statement following the **end case** statement.

It is an extremely useful construct since it gives the programmer a more convenient method of implementing a multi-way choice than is possible with multiple ifs. As an example, let us look at a function which has been implemented using **if** statements:

```
get(operand_type);
if operand_type = single then
    single_mult;
elsif operand_type = double then
    double_mult;
elsif operand_type = complex then
    complex_mult;
elsif operand_type = vector then
    vector_mult;
else
    put("Operand Error");
end if;
```

Below is the same function, this time implemented with a **case** statement:

```
get(operand_type);
case operand_type is
    when single    => single_mult;
    when double    => double_mult;
    when complex   => complex_mult;
    when vector    => vector_mult;
    when others    => put("Operand Error");
end case;
```

The **case** implementation of the function is much easier to read and understand than the multiple **if** statements, and is consequently less prone to programming errors.

The **when** clause is not limited to a single choice. We can 'or' together several possibilities into one choice, or even define a range of values for which we wish a particular action or actions to take place, as in the next two examples:

```
case keyboard_input is
    when                    "0". ."9"        => numeric_convert;
    when   "A". ."Z"    |   "a". ."z"        => alpha_code;
    when   " ". ."/"    |   "<". ."@"
         | "[". ."`"    |   "{ ". ."~"       => special_code;
    when                    others           => control_code;
end case;

case weather is
    when     sunny    =>    shorts;
    when     cloudy   =>    jacket;
    when     raining  =>    coat;
                           umbrella;
    when     snowing  =>    coat;
                           umbrella;
                           hat;
                           boots;
end case;
```

Note that the **others** clause provides a simple mechanism for allowing the programmer to specify all other values of the **case** expression, without having to list them all. It does not mean that the programmer can neglect to specify an action to be performed for *every* possible value of the expression, rather that there is a shorthand way to list the unspecified ones. This is in contrast to some other languages such as Pascal, which require that there be an explicit action listed for every possible value of the expression and is preferable to the Algol-68 "*out*".

2.5 THE GOTO STATEMENT

The **goto** statement in Ada performs the same function as the Algol, Fortran, and Pascal GOTO statements. It allows the programmer to perform an unconditional jump from one place in his program to another. The syntax is:

goto_statement ::= **goto** *label_name*;
lable ::= <<*identifier*>>

The mechanism for identifying the destination of the **goto** is to 'label' the requisite statement. A label is an identifier enclosed in pairs of angled brackets.

This is in direct contrast to Fortran or Pascal labels which must be numeric. A sample program fragment might look like this:

```
        get(x);
        get(y);
        if x = y then
                goto finish;
        else
                process(x,y);
        end if;
        . . .

        . . .
<<finish>> put("All Done.");
```

Since a label is an identifier, it is natural to wonder about its declaration and scope. The resolution lies in the implicit declaration of a label at the end of the declarations for the innermost enclosing body. This defines its scope, and thus its visibility and therefore limits the parts of the program from which a jump may be made.

Note that the programmer is not limited to a single label on a statement; he or she may use as many as are necessary or desirable. Thus, we could have many jumps to differing labels, all of which result in the same statement being the next to be executed.

```
                . . .
                goto finish;
                . . .
<<done>>
<<finish>>
<<way_out>>
                next;
                . . .
                goto way_out;
                . . .
                goto finish;
```

The use of the **goto** is currently an item of controversy, there being differing views about its effect on good programming practices. Some proponents of structured programming methodologies have suggested that it be removed from the language entirely, since any construct which contains a **goto** can be rewritten with **ifs**, **whiles**, etc. to remove it.

The application of structured methodologies and the use of **goto**s are not inherently incompatible, provided that **goto**s are used with care. They are a powerful tool in certain situations, such as panic exits, or places where execution speed is extremely critical, such as an interrupt handler. The penalties incurred in their use outweigh the benefits in all but a vanishingly small number of instances, however, and the use of a **goto** should be avoided unless there is no other alternative. The **goto** is a double-edged sword, and requires a skilled hand to make the best use of it.

2.6 THE RAISE STATEMENT

The **raise** statement is used to indicate that there is an error condition, or **exception**, which requires processing by an 'exception handler'. Its effect is similar to executing a **goto** instead of the **raise**, with the destination being the start of the exception handler. The syntax of the **raise** statement is:

raise_statement ::= **raise** [*exception_name*] ;

The whole issue of exception handling and the **raise** statement will be dealt with in a later chapter. It is mentioned here because it can alter the flow of a program.

CHAPTER 3

Types and Simple Data

As the fields of software and software engineering have evolved, the emphasis in language research has switched from an algorithmic description of a problem (specifying what operations are to be performed) to a data-oriented view (specifying what objects are to be manipulated). This has led to more studies in the areas of data representation and data description, and some of the fruits of these labours are now seeing the light of day in languages such as Ada.

In this chapter we shall expand upon the theme of data representation and description, looking at the Ada concept of 'types'. We shall see how the programmer can define his own types and how to build more complicated types from the simpler ones. It is the ability of the programmer to tailor his data descriptions to fit his own requirements which is one of the most powerful aspects of Ada.

3.1 TYPE DECLARATION

In the previous chapters, we saw how objects of a given built-in type could be declared and could then be used to hold values of that type. There are situations, however, where the built-in types are awkward or insufficient for the job at hand. As an example, it is cumbersome for the programmer to have to remember (and document) that in his program the continents are represented by integer numbers (1=North America, 2=Europe, 3=Asia, etc.). What is really required is a means by which the programmer can create his own types which can then be used to represent data in a manner convenient to him. In Ada, the mechanism which allows you to do this is called 'type declaration', and it is used to introduce a new type to the compiler. Once a new type has been declared, it may then be used for the declarations of objects of that type in the same manner as the built-in types. There is no functional distinction between the built-in and the user-defined types.

The syntax of the type declaration statement is:

type_declaration ::=

      type *identifier* [*discriminant_part*] **is** *type_definition*;

    | *incomplete_type_declaration*

type_definition ::=

      enumeration_type_definition | *integer_type_definition*
    | *real_type_definition* | *array_type_definition*
    | *record_type_definition* | *access_type_definition*
    | *derived_type_definition* | *private_type_definition*

When the programmer defines a new type, he is specifying a particular set of characteristics which will apply to objects of that type. Among these are the valid range of values which an object of that type may take, and the operations which may be performed on or between such objects. The remainder of this chapter and the whole of the next one are devoted to a study of the details of each of the various *type_definitions* and the characteristics that they imply.

3.2 SCALAR AND DISCRETE TYPES

Before we consider the individual *type_definitions,* it will be useful to explore the concepts of 'scalar' and 'discrete' types. A scalar type has the following features:

1. Its values have no components.
2. Its value set is ordered.
3. There is a defined range for the value set.

Ada allows the programmer to determine the range of valid values of a particular scalar type via the attribute enquiry functions. For any scalar type, we can find the minimum and maximum implemented values of that type (*my_type,* for example) by writing:

    my_type'first   minimum value of the type *my_type*
    my_type'last   maximum value of the type *my_type*

A subset of the scalar types are the discrete types. The discrete types consist of the enumeration types and the integer types. Since discrete types have value sets which consist of discrete values, each value has a 'position number' which defines that value's position in the sequence. Similarly, a particular discrete value has a predecessor and a successor (with the obvious exception of the end points). The predecessor and successor of a value may be found by using the enquiry functions:

    my_type'pos(x)   position number of x
    my_type'pred(x)   predecessor to x
    my_type'succ(x)   successor to x

Note: The position number of the 'smallest' value in the valid range is *zero* (*my_type'pos(my_type'first)* = 0)

We shall see how these functions can be used later in the chapter.

To illustrate the foregoing discussion, the predefined types *'fixed'*, *'float'*, *'integer'* and *'character'* are all scalar types, but only *'integer'* and *'character'* are discrete.

3.3 ENUMERATION TYPES

An enumeration type is one whose values consist of an ordered set of discrete values. We have already met examples of enumeration types in Chapter 1 when we were discussing the boolean and character types. The syntax for an enumeration type definition is:

enumeration_type_definition ::=
    (*enumeration_literal* {, *enumeration_literal* })
enumeration_literal ::= *identifier* | *character_literal*

The order in which the literals are given in the *type_definition* is significant, since it defines the relationship of one value to the next. Thus, if we were to define a type to represent the compass points, like this:

type *cardinal* **is** (*north, east, south, west*);

then the relationships between them would be:

north < *east* < *south* < *west*

This ordering is important, since it will affect the outcome of a condition. It is easy to imagine two code fragments, where the algorithm is the same, but the results are different:

```
declare
    type cardinal is (north, east, south, west);
    direction : cardinal; -- define a 'cardinal' variable
begin
    . . .
    direction := south;
    . . .
    if direction < east then
        correct_drift; -- not executed, since south > east
    end if;
end;

declare
    type cardinal is (north, south, east, west);
    direction : cardinal; -- define a 'cardinal' variable
begin
    . . .
    direction := south;
    . . .
```

```
        if direction < east then
            correct_drift; -- executed, since south < east
        end if;
    end;
```

The ability to define your own enumeration types can be extremely useful. In
a text processing application, for example, we might be required to represent
the Greek alphabet for later typesetting. Rather than assign numbers to each
Greek character (1=alpha, 2=beta, etc.), we could define our own type for the
alphabet and then generate and manipulate objects of that type, as in this example:

```
    declare
        type greek is
            (alpha,      beta,        gamma,       delta,     epsilon,    zeta,
             eta,        theta,       iota,        kappa,     lambda,     mu,
             nu,         xi,          omicron,     pi,        rho,        sigma,
             tau,        upsilon,     phi,         chi,       psi,        omega);
        g_char : greek; -- define a variable of type 'greek'
        alt_set : boolean;
    begin
        . . .
        if alt_set then
            read_greek(g_char);
            typeset(g_char);
        end if;
        . . .
    end;
```

There is an added advantage to using a user-defined type rather than a 1,2,3...
system, because it allows the compiler to check for type compatibility. Remember,
Ada does not allow you to mix types within an expression without an explicit
type-conversion. Thus, the compiler can check for possible errors such as the
following:

```
    declare
        line_number :  integer;
        gchar       :  greek;
    begin
        . . .
        line_number := alpha;      -- not allowed, mixed types
        . . .
        line_number := 1;          -- valid if '1' is a line number, and
                                      syntactically valid but logically
                                      incorrect if '1' represents 'alpha'.
    end;
```

The next example illustrates the use of the attribute enquiry functions with an enumeration type:

```
declare
    type hand is (thumb, index, middle, ring, little);
    this_finger      : hand;   -- define a 'hand' object
    this_finger_no   : integer;
    max_fingers      : constant integer :=
                             hand'pos(hand'last); -- 4
begin
    . . .
    read_hand(this_finger);   -- 'thumb', 'index', etc.
    this_finger_no  := hand'pos(this_finger);
    put(this_finger_no); -- '0', '1', etc.
    . . .
end;
```

If you review the sections of Chapter 1 which dealt with the boolean and character types, the manner in which they fit into the scheme of enumeration types should now be readily apparent.

Consider now the circumstance where the programmer has a need to define two (or more) new enumeration types and finds that some of the literals for one type are the same as those of the other, as in this fragment:

```
type body is (head, arms, legs, trunk);
type table is (top, drawers, legs);
```

In a situation like this where a literal can have more than one interpretation, it is said to be 'overloaded'. In Ada it is perfectly acceptable to define types with overloaded literals. However, care is required when using them. When an overloaded literal is used; its type must either be determinable from its context, or the desired type must be explicitly stated using a 'qualified expression' of the form:

```
type'(expression)
```

To illustrate,

```
declare
    type desk is (top, drawers, legs);
    type table is (top, leaves, legs);
begin
    . . .
    write(desk'(legs));     -- qualification required as 'legs'
    . . .                   -- is overloaded.
    write(leaves);          -- no qualification required
    . . .
```

```
    for i in table'(top)     . . legs loop
    . . .                    -- qualification for either 'legs'
    . . .                    -- or 'top' required to determine
    . . .                    -- the type.
    end loop;
end;
```

3.4 INTEGER TYPES

We have already been introduced to the integer types in Chapter 1. However, in many instances of programming, an integer variable is used in a situation where only a small subset of the range of the predefined type *'integer'* is required. Consider the following:

```
declare
    day_number, page_number     : integer;
    number_of_grains            : integer;
begin
    . . .
    read(number_of_grains);        -- 10,000 for example
    day_number := number_of_grains − 3;
    page_number := −273;
    . . .
end;
```

The use of integer variables in these circumstances has one serious drawback. Since all of the variables and all of the literals are of type integer, there are no type incompatibilities, and in the absence of over- or under-flow errors there is no way to check for errors such as a negative *page_number* or a *day_number* of 9,997, either at compile-time or at run-time. What is really required is a mechanism for defining a new integer type with a limited range which would then allow reasonable checking to be performed. The integer *type_definition* achieves this function by allowing the programmer to declare new integer types which are derived from the built-in integer type. Its syntactic definition is:

integer_type_definition ::= *range_constraint*

We can now rewrite the previous example, this time taking advantage of this new feature:

```
declare
    type days is range 1. .366;   -- including leap-years
    type pages is range 1. .5000; -- a reasonable number
    day_number      : days;
    page_number     : pages;
    number_of_grains : integer;
```

begin

    . . .

    read(*number_of_grains*);   – – 10,000 for example

    day_number := *number_of_grains* – 3;

        – – an error would be generated here, as 9,997 is

        – – not in the valid range for an object of type

        – – 'days'.

    page_number := −273;

        – – another error, because a 'pages' object cannot

        – – be negative.

    . . .

end;

Notice that in the rewritten example, there is sufficient information about the individual variables for range checking at both compile- and run-time.

We are not required by the language to limit the range of our new types to be positive. If the situation calls for it, we can define any range we want, subject only to the restrictions that the range cannot be null, nor can it exceed the bounds of the implemented range of the built-in type integer, from which the new type is derived. Bearing these points in mind, all of the following integer *type_declarations* are valid:

type   *tolerance* **is** −20. .20;

type   *sub_zero* **is** −50. .−1;

type *near_absolute* **is** −273. .−230;

type *serial_number* **is** 1. .1000;

Because the newly declared types are derived from the original integer type, they 'inherit' the operators and functions defined for objects of type integer. Thus, it is not necessary to define new ones, even though we are declaring new types.

It is important to note that whenever the programmer uses a type definition he is introducing a *new* type. It is different from all other types, and cannot therefore be mixed with another type in an expression, even if it has identical characteristics, unless the type compatibility rules are followed:

declare

    type *little_int*   **is range** 1. .5;

    type *small_int*   **is range** 1. .5;

    little_var   : *little_int*;

    small_var, tiny_var : *small_int*;

begin

    . . .

    little_var   := 3;

    small_var   := *little_var*;   – – illegal, mixed types

small_var   := *small_int*(*little_var*);
                              -- allowed, because of explicit type
                              -- conversion
      tiny_var   := *small_var*;   -- no conversion required, as
                              -- both *small_var* and *tiny_var* were
                              -- declared using the same type_definition
                              -- and are thus of the same type.
   end;

Note that type conversion is only allowed (and only makes sense) between numeric objects or expressions (including real types), between array types, and between derived types (see Section 3.6).

3.5 REAL TYPES

The real types consist of the floating-point and fixed-point types. We have already encountered the built-in types float and fixed in Chapter 1.

In defining a new real type, we are basically concerned with specifying an accuracy requirement (and possibly a range) for the representation of real numbers. It should come as no surprise, therefore, to find that the real *type_definition* is:

real_type_definition ::= *accuracy_constraint*
accuracy_constraint ::=
    floating_point_constraint | *fixed_point_constraint*

3.5.1 Floating Point Types

For the floating-point types, the accuracy requirement is specified in terms of the number of decimal digits of precision required for the mantissa of the number (when represented in base 10).

floating_point_constraint ::=
    digits *static_simple_expression* [*range_constraint*]

The definition places a lower limit on the accuracy with which objects of the new type will be represented and manipulated. A particular implementation may choose to use an accuracy greater than that required, but if you want to write portable programs, rely only on the accuracy you have asked for and no more. Note that the expression after the reserved word **digits** is a static one, meaning that it must be possible to evaluate it at compile-time. Also, you cannot ask for greater accuracy constraints than that of the predefined type '*float*' (or '*long_float*', if it is implemented). Some examples of floating-point *type_declarations* are:

   type *small_float* **is digits** 5;
   type *mid_float* **is digits** 7 **range** 1.0 . . 1.0E6;
   type   *big_float* **is digits** 10 **range** 0.0 . . 1.0E3;

Objects of type *small_float* can represent numbers with an accuracy of 5 digits, such as 2.7183, 2.7183E5, −27.183E4, etc., while objects of type *mid_float* can represent 3.141593, 31415.93, etc., but not −3.141593 because of the range constraint.

For any floating-point type (*my_float*, for example), there are the following enquiry functions which enable the programmer to determine the details of its implementation:

my_float'**digits**	the maximum (integer) number of decimal digits of accuracy available for an object of that type.
my_float'*mantissa*	the (integer) number of bits in the mantissa.
my_float'*emax*	the "range" of the exponent is +/− *my_float*'*emax*.
my_float'*small*	the smallest positive number of type *my_float*.
my_float'*large*	the largest positive number of type *my_float*.
my_float'*epsilon*	a measure of the 'granularity' of the representation.

If you are going to use these, you would do well to read both the standard for Ada and your local reference manuals for details of floating-point representations.

3.5.2 Fixed Point Types

The definition of the accuracy constraint for the fixed-point type is:

fixed_point_constraint ::=
     delta *static_simple_expression* [*range_constraint*]

It is important to note that although the definition shows that the *range_constraint* is optional, it is only optional for subtype indication (see Section 3.6). It is *required* for a fixed-point type definition, because it is not possible for the compiler to determine the necessary representation for the type unless it knows both the range and the delta.

As was pointed out in Chapter 1, the difference between floating-point and fixed-point types is in the accuracy constraints. For a floating-point type, the accuracy is specified by the number of digits required to hold the numeric value, disregarding the exponent. Thus, a floating-point type which was defined as:

type *s_float* **is digits** 3;

could be used to generate objects which could take values such as 1.23, 123000, 0.000123, because each of these numbers can be rewritten as $0.123Ex$, where $x = 1$, 6 or −3 respectively. The accuracy constraint is relative to the size of the number, i.e. the number of significant figures. For the fixed types, however, the accuracy constraint is absolute, the number of decimal places. Thus, if we were to define a fixed-point type with the following *type_declaration*:

type *s_fixed* **is delta** 0.1 **range** 0.0 . . 2000.0;

then it could take values such as 12.3, 123.0, 1230.0 etc., but could never have a value of 1.23 since this would require an accuracy of 2 decimal places, greater than that defined for the type.

When performing multiplication or division with fixed-point operands, the intermediate results are of an arbitrary (higher) accuracy. An implicit *type_conversion* must therefore be performed on them before they can be assigned to a fixed-point object. To illustrate the point:

```
declare
      type s_fixed is delta 0.1  range −100.0 . . 100.0;
      small     : s_fixed;
begin
      . . .
      small := 2.1;
      small := small + 3.2;   − − small now contains 5.3
      small := small * small;
                        − − The calculated intermediate value was
                        − − 28.09. An error will creep in when this
                        − − is converted to fit into 'small'.
      . . .
end;
```

The possibility of rounding or truncation errors must be borne in mind when considering the use of fixed-point arithmetic.

The attribute enquiry functions for fixed-point types are:

my_type'delta   the accuracy of the type
my_type'actual_delta the implemented *delta*
my_type'large   the largest number of *my_type*

In summary, unless there are strong reasons to use fixed-point arithmetic, it is probably easier and safer to work in floating-point.

3.6 SUBTYPES AND DERIVED TYPES

Now that we have covered the scalar types, we can take a short walk through the garden of 'subtypes' and 'derived types'.

In Ada, we can declare not only 'types', but 'subtypes' as well. A subtype, as its name suggests, is a subset of an existing type. The syntax is given as:

subtype_declaration ::=
      subtype *identifier* **is** *subtype_indication*;

subtype_indication ::= *type_mark* [*constraint*]

type_mark ::= *type_name* | *subtype_name*

constraint ::=
      range_constraint | *accuracy_constraint*
      | *index_constraint* | *discriminant_constraint*

When a subtype is declared, its constraint (if there is one) is evaluated, and the 'base' type and constraint are then associated with the subtype's name. It can then be used to generate new objects of type 'subtype'. This appears to duplicate the function of type declaration, so what is it used for? Well, an object of a given subtype requires no type-conversions when used in an expression which contains objects which belong to the parent or 'base' type. Thus, if we wanted to generate an integer counter to range from 0 to 100, we could write:

declare
    subtype *small_int* **is** *integer* **range** 0 . . 100;
    counter : *small_int*;
    start   : *integer*;
begin

    . . .
    counter := *start*; – – no *type_conversion* needed!
    . . .
end;

The advantages of using subtypes to implement subsets of existing types are in the ease of use for the programmer. Since a subtype declaration does not introducing a new type, the subtype has the same attributes as the base type (with the exception of any constraint imposed by the subtype declaration).

    Note that any constraints in a subtype declaration must be compatible with the base type. You could not, for example, write the following:

type *a* **is** *integer* **range** 1 . . 10;
    subtype *b* **is** *a* **range** 5 . . 12; – – *constraint_error*, 12 > 10

A derived type is similar to a subtype, except that it introduces a *new* type which is derived from an existing type, the properties of the derived type being inherited from the 'parent' type. The definition for a derived type is:

    derived_type_definition ::= **new** *subtype_indication*

When a derived type is defined, the programmer introduces to the compiler a type which has the same properties as the parent type but which is nevertheless a different type. It cannot therefore be mixed with the parent type without an explicit type conversion. When we discussed the declaration of the integer types, we were actually declaring new derived types. Thus,

    type *my_int* **is** **range** 1 . . 10;

is equivalent to a declaration:

    type *my_int* **is** **new** *integer* **range** 1 . . 10;

Some examples of subtype and derived type declarations are:

> **type** *revision_number* **is range** 1 .. 20;
> **type** *old_revs* **is new** *revision*;   -- derived
> **type** *new_revs* **is new** *revision* **range** 15 .. 20   -- derived
> **subtype** *a_rev* **is** *revision* **range** 15. .20   -- subtype

In the examples, *'revision_number'* is a parent type for *'old_revs'* and for *'new_revs'*, and the base type for *'a_rev'*. Note that the three types *'revision'*, *'old_rev'* and *'new_rev'* are distinct types and cannot therefore be mixed in an expression, while *'a_rev'* is a subtype of *'revision'*, and therefore can be mixed with *'revision'* objects, but not with the others.

Note that the use of subtypes and derived types is not limited to the scalar types; they can be used with structured types as well, as we shall see in the next chapter.

CHAPTER 4

Structured Data

4.1 ARRAY TYPES

We now come to the first of the structured types, the array type. An array object can be thought of as a series of sub-objects, all of the same type, each of which can be referenced by an index into the series. Thus, the string object *"abcdef"* can be viewed as an array of objects of type *'character'*, the *'a'* being referenced by an index of 1, say, *'b'* by 2, etc. The concept of an array is common to many languages, including Fortran, Algol, Pascal, etc., and should come as no surprise to most readers. In order to understand how to generate array objects, it is first necessary to investigate the type definition for an array:

> *array_type_definition* ::=
>   **array** (*index* { , *index* }) **of** *component_subtype_indication*
> | **array** *index_constraint* **of** *component_subtype_indication*
>   *index* ::= *type_mark* **range** <>
>   *index_constraint* ::= (*discrete_range* { ,*discrete_range* })
>   *discrete_range* ::= *type_mark* [*range_constraint*] | *range*

The definition shows that we can generate two sorts of array type, the upper one which uses indices and the lower one, which uses index constraints. In Ada, an array type definition of the upper form is called an *'unconstrained array type definition'*, while a definition of the lower form is a *'constrained array type definition'*.

The unconstrained array type definition is used to generate array types where the ranges of the indices (and hence the length of the arrays) are not specified before the fact, and we wish to leave that decision open until we actually generate objects of that type. Thus, we could write:

> **type** *vector* **is array** (*integer* **range** <>) **of** *float*;

which would introduce a type *'vector'*, from which we could generate several *'vector'* objects each with a different length and differing index ranges, but each being one-dimensional and each composed of *'float'* objects.

```
type vector is array (integer range <>) of float;
a :  vector(−1..10); -- index is integer in range − 1 to 10
b :  vector( 0..10); -- same type, different index range
c :  vector( 20..50); --                              ditto
```

Note that the specification of the type of the index was made in the array type declaration, but that the range of the index was left undefined until the object declaration. Any discrete type may be used for an index, allowing us to write:

```
type continent is
    (Africa, Asia, America, Europe, Australia, Antarctica);
type population is array (continent range <>) of integer;
a :  population (Africa..Australia);
```

Obviously, any difference between the type of the index as specified in the type declaration and that of the index constraint in the object declaration will result in an error.

We are not limited to a single index; we can add more if they are necessary, the number of indices being known as the "dimensionality" of an array. Thus, *a, b* and *c* are all one-dimensional arrays. An example of a 2-dimensional array might be:

```
type vector_2d is array
    (integer range <>, integer range <>) of float;
d :  vector_2d(1..20, 1..50);
```

It is important to note that the order of the indices is significant. In the above example, $d(1,2)$ does not reference the same object as $d(2,1)$, and similarly the upper bound of the first index is 20 and that of the second is 50. In other words the indices are position dependent.

Let us now consider the constrained array type definition. In contrast to the unconstrained array type definition which can only be used in type declarations, the constrained array type definition is used for both type- and object-declarations. In fact, all of the examples above used constrained array type definitions in their object declarations. The constrained definition allows us to fix the type and range of the indices as a part of the type or in the object declaration, as follows:

```
type matrix_2d is array
            (integer 1..20, integer 1..50) of float;
e :  matrix_2d; -- bounds fixed by type-definition!
```

We could just as well have declared 'e' without the prior declaration of 'matrix_2d', as in:

```
e :  array (integer 1..20, integer 1..50) of float;
        -- bounds fixed in object declaration.
f :  array (1..20, 1..50) of float;
        -- the type of the range defaults to 'integer'
```

There is no requirement that the bounds of a type or object be given as literals; they can quite validly be variables:

g : **array** (*m . . n, o . . p, q . . r*) **of** *float*;

where the type of the indices, if not specified, is assumed to be integer. An array such as this, in which the bounds are flexible, is called a dynamic array. Note that the type of an index must always be one of the discrete types, since it does not make sense to talk about an array index with a value of, for example, 0.75.

The bounds of an array are determined when the array declaration is elaborated. Thus, if we have a dynamic array, the variables which define its bounds must be visible from the declaration and have valid values when the elaboration takes place.

As with the other types we have met, the array type has attribute enquiry functions. For any array type, *'vec'*, for example, they are:

vec'first	lower bound of first index
vec'last	upper bound of first index
vec'length	number of values in first index
vec'range	subtype defined by the range
	vec'first. . vec'last
vec'first(n)	lower bound of *n'th* index
vec'last(n)	upper bound of *n'th* index
vec'length(n)	number of values of *n'th* index
vec'range(n)	subtype defined by the range
	vec'first(n) . . vec'last(n)

We can illustrate the use of the enquiry functions by considering how we might implement a function to calculate the sum of the elements in a 2-dimensional matrix:

```
function sum (matrix  :  vector) return float is
     temp  : float := 0.0;
begin
     for i in matrix'first . . matrix'last loop
          for j in matrix'first(2) . . matrix'last(2) loop
               temp := temp + matrix(i,j);
          end loop;
     end loop;
     return temp;
end sum;
```

There are certain operations which can be performed on array objects or parts of array objects without necessarily having to manipulate the individual components of the arrays involved. For example, we can initialise or copy all or part of an array, as shown below:

```
declare
     type my_vec is array (1. .10) of integer;
     x, y : my_vec;
begin
     . . .
     x(1. .5)  := 0;  -- assign to 1st 5 elements of x
     x(6. .10):= 1;  --- assign to 2nd 5 elements of x
                        -- x = 0, 0, 0, 0, 0, 1, 1, 1, 1, 1
     y := x;             -- y is now the same as x
     x(1. .3)  := y(7. .9);
                        -- x = 1, 1, 1, 0, 0, 1, 1, 1, 1, 1
     x(4. .5)  := x(1. .2);
                        -- x = 1, 1, 1, 1, 1, 1, 1, 1, 1, 1
end;
```

There is yet another method of assigning to an array, using an aggregate value. An aggregate is a way of describing a value which is made up of components, its syntax being:

aggregate ::=
     (*component_association* { , *component_association* })
component_association ::=
     [*choice* { | *choice* } =>] *expression*

An aggregate value assignment can indicate the correspondence between components of the aggregate and the individual elements of an array in one of three ways, by position, by range, and by index value. The next few examples show the use of various aggregate values for array assignments:

```
declare
     type my_array is array (1. .10) of integer;
     type vector_3 is array (1. .10, 1. .20, 1. .30) of integer;
     a : my_array := (1. .10 => 0); -- all elements set to zero
     b : vector_3; -- no initialisation
begin
     . . .
     a := (1. .5 => 1, 6. .10 => 3);
                -- correspondence found from range, as above
                -- a = 1, 1, 1, 1, 1, 3, 3, 3, 3, 3
     . . .
```

$a := (1,1,2,2,3,3,4,4,5,5)$;
    -- correspondence found from position in sequence

. . .

$a := (1|3|5|7|9 => 1, \textbf{others} => 0)$;
    -- correspondence found from index
    -- $a = 1,0,1,0,1,0,1,0,1,0$

. . .

$b := (1. .10 => (1. .20 =>) (1. .30 => 0)))$;
    -- a 3-D array, therefore the aggregate is given as an 1-D
       aggregate of 2-D components (given as a 1-D array of
       individual components).

. . .

end;

The following rules apply to the use of aggretates for array assignments.

1. When using choices in an aggregate, each choice may appear once and only once.
2. The use of a range in an aggregate is shorthand way of specifying all of the intermediate index values, including the upper and lower bounds of the range.
3. The **others** term may only appear as the last item in the component list.

We shall see a great deal of similarity between the use of aggregates for array assignments and their use with records in section 4.3.

In all our discussions on arrays, we have been talking either of the whole array, or one component of it. Ada provides a third mechanism for accessing arrays, namely the slice. A slice is a one-dimensional array which denotes a subset of an array. To illustrate, if we have an array defined as follows:

type *vector* **is array** $(1. .20)$ **of** *float*;
my_vector : *vector*;

then the following are all slices of *my_vector*:

my_vector$(1. .5)$
my_vector$(1. .19)$
my_vector$(19. .20)$
my_vector$(20. .19)$ -- a null slice, since the index range
                    -- is null (lower bound is predecessor
                    -- of upper bound)

Note that the type of the slice is the base type of the named array.

4.2 THE STRING TYPE

For the programmer's convenience, there is a predefined type *'string'*. This type is equivalent to the type declaration:

> **subtype** *natural* **is** *integer* **range** 1 . . *integer'last*;
> **type** *string* **is array** (*natural* **range** <>) **of** *character*;

A *'string'* object is a 1-dimensional array of *'character'* objects, its length being defined either in the usual manner of arrays or by implication from an initial value assignment.

> *line_buffer*   : *string*(1. .132);
> *blank_buffer* : *string*(1. .132) := (1. .132 =>' ');
> *header*   : **constant** *string* := "*My Sample String.*";
>   --
>   -- Note: A character literal is enclosed by ' and '.
>   -- A string literal is enclosed by " and ".
>   --

As an aside, note that the assignment of an initial value to a string is a special form of the assignment of an aggregate value to an array.

There is one operator which is defined for use between 'string' objects, &, the catenation operator. With this operator we can write:

> *help*   : **constant** *string* := "*Help*";
> *me*   : **constant** *string* := "*Me*";
> *helpme*   : **constant** *string* := *help* & *me;* -- "*HelpMe*"

The relational operators <=, <, >, >= are all defined for strings, the results depending on the lexicographic ordering. As an example, "*a*" is less than "*b*" and similarly "*aa*" is less than "*b*". As with the predefined type *'character'*, this ordering defines a collating sequence.

4.3 RECORD TYPES

Records are similar to arrays in that they are structures composed of "smaller" objects. They differ from arrays, however, in that they may be composed of objects with differing types and that the components may be referenced by name. They are similar in concept to the Cobol Record. The syntax of the record type definition is:

> *record_type_definition* ::=
>   **record**
>   *component_list*
>   **end record**

component_list ::=
    {*component_declaration*} [*variant_part*] | **null**;

component_declaration ::=
    identifier_list : *subtype_indication* [:= *expression*] ;
   | *identifier_list* : *array_type_definition* [:= *expression*] ;

Some examples at this point will illustrate the definition of record types:

type *person* **is**
   record
      surname : *string*(1..20 =>' ');-- default to blanks
      age   : *integer* **range** 0..130;
      gender   : *sex*;   -- female, male
      married : *boolean*;   -- yes, no
   end record;

type *automobile* **is**
   record
      maker   : *manufacturer*;
      colour : *paints*;
      import : *boolean*;
      year   : *integer* **range** 1900..2000;
   end record;

type *address* **is**
   record
      number : *integer* := −1; -- default to −1
      street   : *string*(1..80 =>' '); -- all strings
      town   : *string*(1..80 =>' '); -- default to
      county : *string*(1..80 =>' '); -- blanks.
   end record;

As usual, there must be type compatibility between the component type and the value used for default initialisation of objects of that type, or an error will be generated.

We now know how to generate some record types, but we have yet to learn how to generate record objects or to access and manipulate them. In Ada, the parts of a record are addressed by selecting a "component", the syntax of which is:

selected_component ::=
    name.identifier | name.**all** | *name.operator_symbol*

We can ignore the *name.***all** and *name.operator_symbol* options for now, as they do not apply to records. This leaves us with the simple '*name.identifier*' option for accessing a record component, where '*name*' is the name of the record and *'identifier'* is the component identifier. The next example shows how to declare some record objects, using the type definitions given above, and how to access the components of the newly declared objects:

```
declare
     mary, john    : person;      -- Note: surnames default to blanks
     home, base    : address;     -- ditto for street, town and county
     car           : automobile; -- no defaults for this type
begin
     mary.surname    := "jones";
     john.surname    := mary.surname;
     john.gender     := male;
     car             := (ford, red, false, 1981);
          -- example of record aggregate which uses
          -- positional component correspondance.
     car             := (import => false,
                          colour => red,
                          year   => 1981,
                          maker  => ford);
          -- example of record aggregate which uses
          -- components.
     home.town       := "perth";
     base            := home; -- whole record assignment
end;
```

Note the use of aggregate record values to initialise the whole record. The two examples achieve the same effect but using different mechanisms for deciding the correspondences.

4.3.1 Record Discriminants

In all of the examples so far, we have been dealing with records whose components have fixed lengths. This is inconvenient for the programmer, because it means that he has to know the size of the largest array or string before he can define a record which will work in all cases. What is really required is a means of passing parameters to the record type declaration and allowing the components to then be generated with exactly the required size when a declaration is elaborated. In Ada, this mechanism is the *discriminant_part*. Note that it is a feature of the syntax of the type declaration and does not therefore appear in the syntax of a record type definition. The syntax for discriminants is:

```
discriminant_part ::=
     (discriminant_declaration { , discriminant_declaration })
discriminant_declaration ::=
     identifier_list : subtype_indication [:= expression]
```

Since the discriminants are used to define the length of arrays or strings, they must belong to one of the discrete types. Some examples of the use of discriminants with records are:

```
type family(size : integer) is
    record
        members : array(1..size) of person;
    end record;

type library(shelves, books_per_shelf : integer) is
    record
        volumes : array(1..shelves, 1..books_per_shelf)
                        of book;
    end record;
```

When we make assignments to entire record objects, as opposed to an individual record component, we assign a record value to a record object. For records of fixed size (no discriminants) the record value consisted of the values to be assigned to the components of the record. For a record with a discriminant part, however, the size (and thus the number of components) can vary. The record value for a record with discriminant parts therefore requires the inclusion of the values of any discriminants. To illustrate:

```
declare
    type heading(length : integer range 1..80 := 80) is
        record
            text : string(1..length);
        end record;
    title : heading; -- initial lenght is 80
begin
    ...
    title := (lenght => 5, text => "Title");
                -- aggregate assignment, note the discriminant
                -- comes first.
    ...
end;
```

This example also illustrates how we can place default initial values on the discriminants of a record in the same way that it can be done for variables. The thing to bear in mind is that if you place a default on one discriminant, you must do it for all of them.

4.3.2 Discriminant Constraints
In much the same way that we can place a constraint on the range of an array, for example, we can constrain the range of values of a discriminant. As an

example, suppose we wished to define a record to hold temporarily the contents of a letter. If the average letter is only 3 pages long, we could use that as a default, as follows:

type *letter*(*no_pages* : *integer* **range** 1. . *max_pages* := 3); **is**
    record
        content : **array**(1..*no_pages*) **of** *page;*
    end record;
my_letter : *letter*; -- defaults to 3 pages in length

We can change the constraint on the number of pages by making a record value assignment, but this is rather cumbersome. Instead, we can set the constraint in the object declaration:

his_letter   : *letter*;   -- 3 pages long again
your_letter   : *letter*(15); -- now we have 15 pages
their_letter : *letter*(*no_pages* => 10); -- alternate form of
                                        -- constraint

Note that if there are no default discriminant constraints in the type declaration then we must specify the constraints in every object declaration. If there are defaults, they are overridden by the new constraints. The syntax of a discriminant constraint is:

discriminant_constraint ::=
    (*discriminant_specification* { , *discriminant_specification* })
discriminant specification ::=
    [*discriminant_name* { | *discriminant_name* } =>] *expression*

If an object such as *my_letter* is from a type which has discriminants, there is an attribute enquiry function:

my_letter'constrained

returning a boolean value which enables us to determine whether a discriminant constraint applies to the object. Thus, in the examples above, *his_letter'constrained* would be false and *your_letter'constrained* and *their_letter'constrained* would be true.

4.3.3 Record Variants

In talking about discriminants, we have learned how to alter the size of a component of a record. If you refer back to the syntax definition of a record type definition, you will notice a reference to the optional variant part. This is one of the most useful features of records in Ada, as it gives the programmer the ability to alter which components make up a record rather than the size of a particular component. The syntax is:

variant_part ::=
    case *discriminant_name* **is**
      {**when** *choice* { | *choice* } =>
        component_list }
    end case;

choice ::= *simple_expression* | *discrete_range* | **null**

To see how we might use a variant record, look at the following example :

    type *vehicle* **is** (*bicycle, car, truck*);
    . . .
    type *transport*(*vehicle_style* : *vehicle*) **is**
      record
              owner   : *string*(1. .80);
           description : *string*(1. .80);
           case *vehicle_stype* **is**
             when   *car* => *licence* : *string*(1. .80);
             when *truck* => *licence* : *string*(1. .80);
                                trailer : *boolean*;
             when others => **null**;
        end case;
      end record;

This record type will have differing numbers of components, depending on the *vehicle_style* parameter. We could use the above type declaration to generate and initialise the following three record objects:

    declare
      my_truck   : *transport*(*trucks*);
      my_car   : *transport*(*car*);
      my_bicycle : *transport*(*truck*);
    begin
      . . .
      my_truck   := ("*John Smith*", "*Truck*", "1ALC261", *false*);
      my_car   := (*owner* => "*John Smith*",
                      description => "*Car*",
                      licence => "MA3785");
      my_bicycle := ("*John Smith*", "*Bicycle*");
      . . .
    end;

Note that from this type declaration we can define some subtypes, if we wish:

    subtype *bike* **is** *transport*(*bicycle*);
    subtype *auto* **is** *transport*(*car*);
    subtype *camion* **is** *transport*(*truck*);

which could then be used in object declarations without having to specify the variant part. Any such objects would then automatically have the attributes which the subtype inherited from its parent type, *'transport'*.

4.4 ACCESS TYPES AND ALLOCATORS

In all of the preceding treatments of object declarations, it has been an implicit assumption that whenever an object declaration is elaborated, memory space appropriate for an object of the given type is allocated, and at the same time the identifier in the declaration is associated with that part of memory. An object which is generated in this manner is accessible from wherever it is visible from another portion of the program, this depending on the lexical structure of the program. The structure of the program text is not dynamic, and does not depend on the execution of the resulting code in any way. It therefore follows that the objects we have discussed cannot have been dynamic either; their *'existence'* depends only on the static properties of the program text.

There are circumstances in which the programmer may not know in advance how the correspondence between an identifier and an object should be determined, for example in a situation where he is accessing one of several buffers. What is really wanted is a mechanism for defining a name for an object, but leaving the actual object associated with the name unresolved until the program runs. In Ada these functions are performed by using access types and allocators.

In the same way that integer objects can take on any value from the range of integers, an access object can take values from the set of access values. When an allocator is executed, it generates a object of the required type, allocates storage for it, and returns an access value. This may be assigned to an access object, and thus is forged the link between dynamically created objects and the references to them.

The syntax definition for access types and allocators is:

access_type_definition ::= **access** *subtype_indication*

incomplete_type_declaration ::=
      type *identifier* [*discriminant_part*] ;

allocator ::=
      new *type_mark* [(*expression*)]
  | **new** *type_mark aggregate*
  | **new** *type_mark discriminant_constraint*
  | **new** *type_mark index_constraint*

To see how these work, let us follow the sequence of events in the next example:

declare
      type *pool_space* **is array** (1. .5) **of** *integer*;
        --

-- First, lets define the type of the objects we want to
-- dynamically create.
--

type *pool_space_pointer* **is access** *pool_space*;
--

-- This has created an access type, *pool_space_pointer*;
-- which can now be used to create
-- access objects for objects of type *pool_space*.
--

spare : *pool_space_pointer*;
--

-- We now have an access object, whose default
-- initial value is **null**, meaning that it has no
-- value. It can now be used to access *pool_space*
-- objects.
--

pool_element : *pool_space_pointer* := **new** *pool_space*;
--

-- The execution of the allocator '**new** *pool_space*'
-- generated a *pool_space* object and returned an
-- access value for it which was then assigned to
-- the access object *pool_element*.
--

We can now generate access objects for a particular type, we can use an allocator
to generate those objects, and we can assign the access value to an access variable.
We have yet to determine how to get at an access object's value. Before we can
proceed, the distinction between the value held by the access object and the
value which it references must be understood. For non-access objects, when the
programmer writes an identifier in a program, the compiler will ensure that he
references the desired value held by the designated object. For example, if you
were to write "$X := Y$;" in a program, it would be interpreted as "replace the
value represented by the identifier X with the value currently represented by
Y. This is effective because it is assumed that X and Y are direct references
to the actual data objects generated with the declarations of X and Y.

For access variables, the story is a little more complex. If X and Y are
declared as access objects, their values are not directly associated with data
objects. With access objects, the identifiers are used to get to the access value
they represent, which in its turn is used to get to the object which holds the
data we want to manipulate. Thus, while "$X := Y$;" will certainly replace the
contents of X with the contents of Y, the effect is not the same. If X and Y
are access objects, each of which is currently used to access a data object,
then the statement "$X := Y$;" will result in X and Y both accessing the "Y"
data object, and nobody accessing the "X" object, which is now lost.

To achieve the results we want, namely to transfer the contents of the data accessed by "*Y*" to the data object accessed by "*X*", Ada has the component selector **all** (see section 4.3). The next example highlights the use of **all** and illustrates the difference between access values and the data they represent:

declare

      type *get_at_integers* **is access** *integer*; -- access type
      x : *get_at_integers* := **new** *integer* -- access variable
      y : *get_at_integers* := **new** *integer* --- access variable
      a : *integer*

begin

      . . .
      a := 1;   -- assign to a normal variable
      x. **all** := 5;   -- assign to an access variable
      y. **all** := *a*;   --   ditto
      x := *y*;   -- *x* now references *y*'s object
      y. **all** := −1;
      a := *x* .**all**;   -- *a* is now −1!

The wording of the previous few paragraphs may, on first reading, seem a little clumsy. This can be justified by a conscious effort to avoid the use of the word "pointer", used in languages such as Pascal and PL/1. Pointers carry with them implementation details (such as address range, etc.) which do not belong in a discussion of access variables. The Ada language does not specify how the access mechanism is to be implemented, and its explanation in terms of "pointers" could be misleading.

The access type is the last of the types to be covered in this chapter. Private types will be covered in Chapter 6 when we discuss packages.

CHAPTER 5

Subprograms

This chapter is devoted to a study of procedures and functions, known in Ada as subprograms, and a concept which is common to almost all modern languages which are in current use, such as Fortran, Algol, Pascal, Basic, etc.

5.1 PROCEDURES AND FUNCTIONS

Procedures and functions can be thought of as ways of encapsulating a particular portion of code such that it may be invoked at run-time from many places without requiring that there be multiple copies of that code in existence. This is in direct contrast to the classical concept of a macro, which, when expanded at each macro call (at compile-time), causes a copy of the text of the macro to replace the macro call. Although the Ada language does not support macros, the programmer has the option of requesting that particular subprogram bodies be expanded at every call, by using:

pragma *inline* (*subprogram_name* { ,*subprogram_name* });

In order to make subprograms generally useful, a procedure or function may optionally be passed parameters on each invocation, or "call", telling it what data is to be processed and where to put any results.

Before we can use a subprogram or function, we must know what the calling conventions are, that is: the number of parameters, their type and whether this is a procedure or function. An example of the definition of a procedure might be:

procedure *double_an_integer*(*i* : **in out** *integer*) **is**
begin
    i := *i* + *i* ;
end *double_an_integer*;

which declares a procedure called *'double_an_integer'* requiring one parameter of type integer which can be modified by the procedure. It also defines the calculation to be performed when the procedure is called. An example of a call to the above procedure might look like this:

    count := 3;   -- count assumed to be 'integer'
                                   --
    double_an_integer(count);   -- 'call' the procedure
    put(count);   -- count = 6 here

Procedures and functions differ in several respects. The most important one is that functions return a value at the place from which they are called while procedures do not. Functions can also be called as a part of a statement, whereas a procedure call is a statement in its own right and finally, procedures can modify their parameters (if the programmer allows) but functions can only affect the calling program via the returned value. Functions and procedures fulfil similar needs, but differ in the scope of their effects on the caller's environment.

Note that the example given above did not require the use of a procedure. We could have performed the same calculation just as well (and perhaps better, from a stylistic point of view) with a function instead of a procedure, as in the following:

    function double_an_integer(x : integer) **return** integer **is**
    begin
        return x + x ;
    end double_an_integer;

with a call like this:

    count := 3;   -- count assumed to be 'integer'
                                   --
    count := double_an_integer(count);
                                   --
    put(count);   -- count = 6 here;

It is important to note the difference in the effects of the two calls. In the procedure call statement:

    double_an_integer(count);

the value of 'count' was directly modified by the calculations performed "inside" the procedure, when it was called. Contrast this with the statement:

    count := double_an_integer(count);

where the value of 'count' was *not* modified by the function itself, but by the assignment of the value returned by the function to the variable 'count'.

This distinction is most important. The compiler, in restricting the parameters of a function to mode **in**, ensures that the only way for it to affect the calling environment is via the returned value.

5.2 DEFINING A SUBPROGRAM — THE SUBPROGRAM BODY

When the programmer defines a subprogram, he must specify two things to the compiler, the code to perform the actual calculations and a definition of what the subprogram looks like to a calling program. The *subprogram_body* specifies both of these pieces of information at the same time, its syntax being:

subprogram_body ::=
    subprogram_specification **is**
        declarative_part
    begin
        sequence_of_statements
    [**exception**
        { *exception_handler* }]
    end [*designator*] ;

subprogram_specification ::=
    procedure *identifier* [*formal_part*]
    | **function** *designator* [*formal_part*] **return** *subtype_indication*

formal_part ::= (*parameter_declaration* {; *parameter_declaration* })

parameter_declaration ::=
    identifier_list : *mode subtype_indication* [:= *expression*]

mode ::= [**in**] | **out** | **in out**

designator ::= *identifier* | *operator_symbol*

The *subprogram_specification* defines for the compiler the appearance of the procedure or function from the calling program's point of view, and the appearance of the call, from the subprogram's point of view. It is thus a definition of the interface between the subprogram and the rest of the system. The remainder of the subprogram body specifies the mechanics of the calculations to be performed and any special requirements for exception handling. This is the part enclosed in the **begin** . . . **end,** given in the syntax definition. Let us start our investigations with a look at the definition of subprogram parameters.

5.2.1 Formal Parameters

If you take a look at the syntax definition for a subprogram body, you will find that the function of the "*formal_part*" of the subprogram specification is to define the parameters of the subprogram. The parameters which are defined in a subprogram body or subprogram declaration are called the 'formal parameters', while those which are given in a call to a subprogram are known as the 'actual parameters'. The *formal_part* specifies the names by which the formal parameters are to be known inside the body of the subprogram, their types and constraints, whether a particular parameter is to be read-only (**in**), which is the default mode if no mode is explicitly stated, write-only (**out**), or read-write (**in out**), and any default initial values. The following are examples of some subprogram specifications, showing various modes of formal parameters:

 procedure *bubble_sort*(*matrix* : **in out** *array*)
  --
  -- Sort an array

 procedure *date*(*day* : **out** *day_of_week*;
      month : **out** *month_of_year*;
       year : **out** *years_ad*   )
  --
  -- Return today's date

 procedure *enqueue* (*item* : **in** *queue_item*;
      this_queue : **in out** *queue*;
      queue_full : **out** *boolean*)
  --
  -- Place a *'queue_item'* object onto a queue

 procedure *dequeue* (*item* : **out** *queue_item*;
      this_queue : **in out** *queue* ;
      queue_empty : **out** *boolean*)
  --
  -- Remove an item from a queue

 function *queue_empty* (*this_queue* : *queue*) **return** *boolean*
  --
  -- Test for an empty queue
  -- Note; no need to specify mode, as functions can
  -- only have parameters of mode **in**.

 function *random_int* (*seed* : **in** *integer* := 31415) **return** *integer*
  --
  -- random number function
  -- Note: mode specification not required, but does no
  -- harm, and is beneficial if it aids clarity
  -- and/or readability.

Let us now try our hand at writing a simple procedure or function to find the maximum in an array of integers:

 procedure *max_int*(*list* : **in** *vector*;
      max : **out** *integer*) **is**
  --
  -- Define a procedure called *'max_int'*, with

```
        -- 2 formal parameters; 'list' of type 'vector',
        -- read-only, and 'max' of type 'integer' and
        -- write-only.
        --
    begin
        --
        -- This is the start of the code to perform the
        -- calculation. The preceding 'begin' marks the
        -- end of the declarative part.
        --
        max := list(list'first);
        for i in list'range loop
            if list(i) > max
            then max := list(i);
            end if;
        end for;
        --
        -- This is the end of both the code and the procedure
        -- body.
        --
    end max_int;
```

The calling program for this procedure might look something like this:

```
    declare
        type vector is array (1 .. 10) of integer;
        my_vec    : vector;
        maximum : integer;
    begin
        ...
        my_vec := (1, 2, 3, 4, 5, 6, 7, 8, 9, 0);
        ...
        max_int(my_vec, maximum);
        put(maximum);  -- "9"
        ...
    end;
```

5.3 ACTUAL PARAMETERS AND SUBPROGRAM CALLS

In all of the foregoing, there has been an implicit assumption that the mechanism for making the association between the actual parameters in the call and the formal parameters in the subprogram definition is a one-to-one correspondence between the two lists, with the first parameter in one list being matched to the first in the other, the second with the second, and so on. While this is certainly valid in Ada, the language also allows the programmer the option of making the association explicit by naming the parameters in a call, using the names from the formal parameter list. Thus, given the following procedure definition:

procedure *delete_file*
        (*file_name*   : *file*;
          volume_name : *volume*;
          password   : *key*;
            owner   : *user*;   ) **is** ...

the following calls are all equivalent:

delete_file (*my_file, my_volume, my_key, me*);

delete_file (*file_name*   => *my_file*,
          volume_name => *my_volume*,
          password => *my_key*;
          owner   => *me*   );

delete_file (*my_file, my_volume, owner* => *me*,
                  password => *my_key*);

All of the foregoing information is given in the syntax definition for a procedure or function call:

procedure_call ::=
    procedure_name [*actual_parameter_part*] ;

function_call ::=
    function_name actual_parameter_part | *function_name* ( )

    actual_parameter_part ::=
        (*parameter_association* {, *parameter_association* })

    parameter_association ::=
        [*formal_parameter* =>] *actual_parameter*

    formal_parameter ::= *identifier*

    actual_parameter ::= *expression*

It is interesting to note that there is a great deal of similarity between the syntax of the *formal_parameter* in the *parameter_association* and the syntax use of named components for record aggregates. As with the record aggregates, subprogram parameters can use a purely position dependant association, a purely named association or a mixture of the two. If they are mixed, then all positional parameters must appear before any named parameter, and the use of the first named parameter requires *all* subsequent parameters to be named.

5.4 PARAMETER MODES AND DEFAULT INITIAL VALUES

If you look back at the example of the function *'random_int'*, you will see that
the parameter has an initial value. This is a useful feature of Ada, whereby the
programmer can specify the default value for any parameter whose mode is **in**. If
a default has been supplied, the corresponding actual parameter may be omitted
from the call, in which case the default value is used in its place. If the parameter
is given in the call, the value of the actual parameter overrides the default value.
As an example of a default actual parameter, the next example uses a default
device:

```
procedure standard_output (    data  : in line;
                               unit  : in device := tty;
                               status  : out boolean    ) is
begin
    . . .
end;

standard_output ( line_buffer, status => fail_flag );
    --
    -- uses default, unit = tty
    --

. . .
standard_output ( line_buffer, printer, fail_flag );
    --
    -- overrides default, unit = printer
    --

. . .
standard_output ( data    => line_buffer,
                  unit    => mag_tape,
                  status  => fail_flag    );
    --
    -- overrides default, unit = mag_tape
    --
```

There are two important points to note about default parameters. Firstly, if an
actual parameter is omitted from a procedure or function call, allowing the
default value to take its place, then all subsequent actual parameters *must* be
named (because the compiler needs to be able to distinguish between a legitimate
parameter omission and a possible programming slip). Secondly, defaults are
only allowed with parameters whose mode is **in**. The compiler will flag any
attempt to put a default value on an **out** or **in out** parameter.

While we are on the subject of parameter modes, it is worth investigating
the effects of the different modes on the passed parameters. The syntax of the
subprogram call allows an expression to be passed to a procedure or function.

If an expression is associated with an **in** parameter, then its value is determined prior to the call. If the formal parameter specifies a mode of **out** or **in out,** then the expression is limited to a variable or a type-conversion of a variable. We are thus able to write the following:

procedure *x* (*y* : **in out** *float*) **is** . . .

declare
    i : *integer*;
begin

   . . .
    x(*float*(*i*));
   . . .
end;

where the value of the integer *'i'* is first converted to an object of type *'float'*, the *float'd* object passed as a parameter to the called procedure. On return from the subprogram, a reverse type conversion from *'float'* back to *'integer'* is performed before copying back to the actual parameter.

As a final word on parameters, the usual checks are applied with regard to type compatibility between the actual parameters in the call and the formal parameters in the specification. Similarly, there are checks for constraints on the parameters, ensuring that any actual parameter passed to the subprogram conform to any requirements of the formal parameters and that any returned parameters or values fit the constraints enforced by the calling program.

5.5 SUBPROGRAM DECLARATIONS

In following the Ada concept of declaring things before they are used, Ada provides the programmer with the ability to declare a subprogram's definition without simultaneously giving the subprogram body. This has several advantages, for readability, for automatic document extraction systems and most importantly, for making a procedure or function in a package available to other users. It allows declarations of related subprograms to be grouped together in a single place, reducing the chances for errors of omission and making it easier to find a particular declaration. The syntax for a subprogram declaration is:

subprogram_declaration ::= *subprogram_specification*
  | *generic_subprogram_declaration*
  | *generic_subprogram_instantiation*
subprogram_specification ::=
    procedure *identifier* [*formal_part*]
  | **function** *designator* [*formal_part*] **return** *subtype_indication*
formal_part ::= (*parameter_declaration* {;*parameter_declaration*})

parameter_declaration ::=
     identifier_list : *mode subtype_indication* [:= *expression*]
mode ::= [**in**] | **out** | **in out**
designator ::= *identifier* | *operator_symbol*
operator_symbol ::= *character_string*

Let us take as an example a package for handling matrix calculations. We can use
the subprogram declaration feature to declare all of the functions and procedures
in the visible part of the package, whilst leaving the corresponding subprogram
bodies in the hidden part. The declarations in the visible part will enable programs
external to the package to determine the calling conventions for the subprograms
but will prevent them from determing what has been done to implement any
particular feature. Thus, we might have a series of declarations:

```
package matrix_calculations is
     procedure mat_add (x, y  :   in matrix;
                             z  : out matrix );
     procedure mad_sub (a, b  :   in matrix;
                             c  : out matrix );
end;

package body matrix_calculations is
     . . .
begin
     . . .
end;
```

which will declare a package to perform matrix addition and subtraction. The
only parts of the package which the calling program can know about are the
two procedure specifications. The actual implementation of the procedures is
hidden in the package body. To use the package, the calling program would
require a **use** cause like this:

```
declare
     use matrix_calculations;
     a, b, c  : matrix;
begin
     . . .
     mat_add (a, b, c);
     . . .
end;
```

The **use** clause causes the entities in the visible part of the package to become
accessible. It will be discussed further in the next chapter, on packages.
     Finally, it should be remembered that if you use a subprogram declaration
and define the subprogram body later on, there is the obvious requirement that

the subprogram declaration and the subprogram specification must agree with each other.

5.6 OVERLOADED SUBPROGRAMS

In much the same way that enumeration literals can have more than one interpretation, depending on their context, subprograms can also be overloaded. This is a useful feature when the programmer has several different objects, each of which can have the same logical function performed on it. As an example, the function *'next_item'* might return a *queue_time,* the next item in a list or the item at the next cursor position on a CRT screen. We could envision a series of declarations:

```
function next_item ( q : queue ) return queue_item is . . .
function next_item ( l  : list    ) return    list_item is . . .
function next_item ( c  : cursor ) return screen_item is . . .
```

with the determination of which function to invoke being resolved at the call. This resolution depends upon there being some distinguishing characteristics in the call which uniquely define only *one* function. The factors used in the determination are the number, order and types of the parameters in the call and in the case of functions, the type of the returned value. If the call does not define one and only one subprogram, then it is said to be ambiguous, and is therefore illegal.

The use of the same subprogram name in an outer and an inner declarative part does not necessarily mean that the declaration of the subprogram in the outer layer is 'hidden' from the inner layer. Hiding only takes place if both declarations introduce subprograms with the same number of parameters, the parameters having the same names, the same types, being in the same order and the same ones having default values. In the case of functions, the type of the results must also be the same. If all of these conditions are met, then the two subprograms are said to be 'equivalent', and the outer one is hidden. Note that the values of any constraints on the parameters, of any initial values and the modes of the parameters are not used in the determination of equivalency.

```
declare
     procedure a ( x : integer );
     function   b ( y : co_ordinate ) return real;
     procedure c ( z : in boolean );
begin
     . . .
     declare
         procedure a ( x : integer );
         - -
```

-- Hides outer $'a'$, because neither the names nor
-- the types are different.
--
function b (y : *co_ordinate*) **return** *co_ordinate*;
--
-- Does not hide outer $'b'$, because the types of
-- the parameters are different.
--
procedure c (z : **in out** *boolean*);
--
-- Hides outer $'c'$, because modes of parameters
-- are not considered in determining hiding.
--
      end;
   end;

If there is a problem with an unwanted hiding, it can usually be resolved by using qualifiers to more explicitly fix either the parameters or the subprogram names.

5.7 OVERLOADED OPERATORS

One of Ada's most powerful features, in common with languages such as Algol-68, is the ability of the programmer to "define" operators for his own types. This is done by defining an function which acts as an operator. Ada allows you to define functions whose names correspond to the predefined language operator designators (with the exception of the operator "/=", as noted below).

logical_operator	::= **and** | **or** | **not**
relational_operator	::= < | <= | = | /= | >= | >
adding_operator	::= + | − | &
unary_operator	::= + | − | **not**
multiplying_operator	::= * | / | **mod** | **rem**
exponentiating_operator	::= **

For the monadic or 'unary' operators, the function can only have one parameter. Thus, for colours we could define the following:

function "+" ($c1, c2$: *colour*) **return** *colour* **is** . . .
function "−" ($c1, c2$: *colour*) **return** *colour* **is** . . .
function "=" ($c1, c2$: *colour*) **return** *boolean* **is** . . .

and use them in the following way:

    x := "+" (*red,blue*)   -- purple, *'red'* corresponding to
                                      -- the formal parameter *'c1'* and
                                      -- *'blue'* to *'c2'*.

    y := "−" (*x,red*);   -- *blue*

    if "/=" (*y, blue*) **then** . . .

Note that the operator "=" must return a boolean result and that its definition also fixes the definition of the operator "/=", which cannot therefore be over-loaded. This operator is also special in that it can only take parameters of a **limited private** type. We shall say more about these in the chapter on packages.

CHAPTER 6

Packages

This chapter is devoted to an exploration of one of the most powerful features of the Ada language, packages, and their effects on the visibility rules.

6.1 OVERVIEW

The notion of encapsulating a part of a program is not new to computer science. The most obvious examples from previous languages are the Fortran subroutine and the Algol or Pascal procedure. These constructs can be used to provide a clean break between a logical function to be performed (taking the square-root of a positive number, for example) and its implementation details (the actual algorithm used, its accuracy, etc.). A similar division is available through the use of libraries of subroutines or procedures (statistics libraries and mathematical libraries are good examples). Unfortunately, neither of these approaches addresses the problems of hiding unnecessary information from the programmer, nor do they adequately prevent him from taking advantage of implementation details at the expense of portability and, potentially, reliability. As an example, let us consider a generalised terminal driver subroutine, written in a language such as Fortran. Let us say that the value of one of its parameters, ITERM, identifies the particular terminal type, 0=TTY, 1=CRT, 2=Graphics CRT, etc. There is no way to hide from the programmer the fact that terminal characteristics are represented by integers, since this information is required in order to make use of the routine.

In Ada, the original idea of encapsulation has been generalised to create the concept of a 'package', whose properties are such that it may encapsulate data, types, algorithms, and combinations of all three. Appropriate mechanisms are provided in the language to ensure that a program only has access to those parts of a package which the programmer has explicitly allowed, and preventing access to all others. The programmer thus has control over which pieces of information from his package are available to users of the package. The package concept is a major step forward in the attempt to provide implementation independent code, and thus towards the goal of portability.

In Ada, a package consists of two parts, the package specification, which defines those entities to which the external world has access, and the package body which contains the code, data, types etc. to perform the desired functions but about which the external world can have no knowledge. A package does not need a body, if all of the information can be given in the specification (see section 6.2.1), nor is there any requirement that a package body be given at the same place as the specification (the two may even be compiled as separate units).

6.2 DEFINING A PACKAGE

As with all other Ada objects, a package needs to be declared before it can be used, via the *package_declaration* whose syntax is as follows:

```
package_declaration ::= package_specification;
    | generic_package_declaration
    | generic_package_instantiation

package_specification ::=
    package identifier is
        { declarative_item }
    [ private
        { declarative_item }
        { representation_specification }]
    end [identifier]
```

and similarly, the body of the package must be defined, its syntax being:

```
package_body ::=
    package body identifier is
        declarative_part
    [ begin
        sequence_of_statements
    [ exception
        { exception_handler }] ]
    end [identifier] ;
```

Note that the package identifier given in the package body must be identical to identifier of the corresponding package specification. Similarly, the optional identifier after the ends must match the one given in the specification and body.

6.2.1 The Package Specification
As mentioned above, the only part of the package about which the external world can have any knowledge is that which is given in the package specification. In Ada, it is called the 'visibile' part of the package. Any object declared in the visible part of a package specification is accessible to a program unit which includes the specification. Some examples of package specifications might be:

```
package complex_arithmetic is
    type complex is
        record
            real_part  : float := 0.0;
            imag_part : float := 0.0;
        end record;
        function "+"  (a, b : complex) return complex;
        function "−"  (a, b : complex) return complex;
        function "*"  (a, b : complex) return complex;
        function "/"  (a, b : complex) return complex;
        function sqr  (a, b : complex) return complex;
end complex_arithmetic;
```

```
package keyboard is
    type key is private;
    function get_key return key;
    function convert_key (a : key) return key;
private
    type key is integer range 0 . . 255;
end keyboard;
```

The first example, the *complex_arithmetic* package, consists of a type declaration which can be used to generate 'complex' objects and the specifications for the overloaded operators +, −, * and / which may be used to manipulate 'complex' objects. It provides the user with the information necessary to perform calculations with complex objects (albeit primitive, since it lacks any operators which would allow scalar operations).

The second example is similar, in that it also contains a type declaration and a number of function declarations. It differs from the *complex_arithmetic* package, however, in the restrictions imposed on the type 'key' by the **private** clause (see section 6.3).

The entire concept of a package is that it may be used without regard to the implementation details which are hidden within its body, so it seems appropriate that the next example should demonstrate how the *complex_arithmetic* package is accessed from a user program, before we delve into the details of the definition of the package body. We'll give an example and then discuss its features.

```
declare
    x, y, z : complex_arithmetic . complex;
begin
    . . .
    z := complex_arithmetic . sqr(x, y);
    . . .
end;
```

We shall assume that the package specification is visible from an outer block of the program, so that it is also visible from this inner one. In this example, the type declaration for *'complex'* is used to generate three complex variables, *x, y,* and *z.* These can then be manipulated with the (overloaded) operators or functions which are similarly declared in the package specification. Remember, there is no reason why the programmer needs to know the details of how the types or functions are implemented. The arithmetic operator "+", for instance, could be implemented as a software subprogram, as a series of hardware instructions, or even as a single instruction to some vector processing hardware.

6.2.2 The Use Clause
Up to this point, we have said little or nothing about the rules which govern the access to objects defined in a package specification, by a user program. To make use of the objects named in the package, we have to make use of selected components (in the same way that record components are selected), by writing statements such as:

    x : *complex_arithmetic . complex*;

which states that the object *'x'* is to be of a type *'complex'*, the type definition being found in the package *'complex_arithmetic'*. In fact, any of the items declared in the package specification must be selected by preceding the object name with the package name and a dot. This can quickly become a troublesome and unnecessary burden, so Ada provides the **use** clause, whose syntax is:

    use_clause ::= **use** *package_name* { , *package_name* };

as a convenience which allows the items declared in a package specification to become directly visible, as if the definitions from the package specification had been written in place of the **use.** We can now rewrite the previous example, taking advantage of this new feature:

```
declare
    use complex_arithmetic;
    x, y, z : complex;
begin
    . . .
    z := sqr(x, y);
    . . .
end;
```

After the **use** clause, the programmer no longer has to give the package name for every object in the package which he wishes to access. This feature is extremely useful, as program readability and documentation tend to be the first things to suffer when a programmer becomes tired of writing or typing long names.

By way of example, contrast the following two program fragments. Both perform the same function, the first the hard way:

declare
> **use** *complex_arithmetic*;
> *x, y, z* : *complex*;

begin
> . . .
> *z* := *sqr(x, y)*;
> *complex_arithmetic_input_output* . *put(z)*;
> . . .

end;

and the second the more sensible way:

declare
> **use** *complex_arithmetic,*
> > *complex_arithmetic_input_output*;
> *x, y, z* : *complex*;

begin
> . . .
> *z* := *sqr(x, y)*;
> *put(z)*;
> . . .

end;

Some caution is required when using this feature, because employment of the **use** clause can lead to ambiguities which can *only* be resolved with component selection. It is easy to conceive of two packages, both of which contain a declaration of the same identifier:

package *person* **is**
> . . .
> *age* : *integer*;

end *person*;
package *antique* **is**
> . . .
> *age* : *integer*;

end *antique*;
. . .
declare
> **use** *person, antique*;
> – – there are now two versions of the variable "age"
> – – available to the programmer.
> *temp* : *integer*;

```
begin
    . . .
    temp := age;              -- illegal, requires more definition
    temp := person . age;   -- ok, not ambiguous any more
    antique . age := temp;-- ok, not ambiguous
    . . .
end;
```

6.2.3 The Package Body

We now come to the package body. This is the part of the package which contains the implementation details of the entities defined in the package specification, the linkage between the specification and the body being the common package name. As an example, the package body for the *complex_arithmetic* package might look something like this:

```
package body complex_arithmetic is
    function "+" (a, b : complex) return complex is
        c : complex;
    begin
        c . real_part := a . real_part + b . real_part;
        c . imag_part := a . imag_part + b . imag_part;
        return c;
    end "+";
    function "−" (a, b : complex) return complex is . . . end;
    function "*" (a, b : complex) return complex is . . . end;
    function "/" (a, b : complex) return complex is . . . end;
    function sqr  (a, b : complex) return complex is . . . end;
end complex_arithmetic;
```

The only access which a user program has to the objects defined in the package body is via the visible part of the package specification. It can be thus seen that the package concept provides the mechanisms required to prevent the programmer from knowing anything about the details of the inner workings of a package. To illustrate, let us consider a package with the following package specification:

```
package trig is
    . . .
    function sine (theta : radians) return float;
    . . .
end trig;
```

The only information about the *'sine'* subprogram available to the user of this package is the calling sequence and the types of any parameters. Because of this, the only things the programmer can ever know about *sine* are the range and accuracy of the returned parameter (found by using the attribute enquiry functions on the type). He cannot determine the algorithm used to find the sine, nor, for example, whether the subprogram uses any intermediate storage. From the programmer's point of view, so long as he can take sines, he need not know whether the sine is calculated by a series approximation, by a table look-up, or even by magic.

As was mentioned in the introduction, there is no requirement for there to be a package body for every package specification. If a specification contains only types or data, objects which can be completely defined in the specification, then there is no need to provide a corresponding package body. In this manner, for example, global constants and global data areas can be defined, and concepts such as Fortran COMMON can be implemented.

```
package common is
        real_common  : array (1..100) of float;
      integer_common  : array (1..100) of integer;
end common;
package terminals is
      type term is private;
private
      type term is (tty, crt, graphic_crt, printer);
      for term use (         tty => 1,
                             crt => 2,
                     graphic_crt  => 3,
                         printer   => 4 );
end terminals;
package document_printer_defaults is
      lines_per_page      : constant integer := 66;
      columns_per_line   : constant integer := 80;
      paper_width    : constant float :=   8.5; -- inches
      paper_length   : constant float := 11.0; -- inches
      header_margin   : constant integer := 3; -- lines
      footer_margin   : constant integer := 8; -- lines
end document_printer_defaults;
```

Each of the above packages can stand on its own, requiring no corresponding package body.

We now come to the concept of package initialisation. In the syntax definition of the package body, there is provision for a sequence of statements to be executed, but before we delve into this, it is necessary to understand what happens during the elaboration of a package body. When a package body is elaborated, the package identifier is introduced and the declarative part is then elaborated, introducing and initialising any variables. Once this has taken place, the sequence of statements in the body is executed. The ability to execute these statements proves to be extremely useful for performing any initialisations which cannot be performed in the declarative part. It is easy to conceive of a job which requires one or more queues to be used. The initial linking of the *queue_ items* onto the *free_item* queue is difficult to perform using only the variable initialisation mechanisms, but easily accomplished using executable statements:

```
package body queue_manager is
    free_queue_size : constant := 100;
    free_item_pool : array (1 . . free_queue_size) of queue_item;
    procedure enqueue (x :   in queue_item) is . . . end;
    procedure dequeue (x : out queue_item) is . . . end;
begin
    -- code to set up initial queue pointers and
    -- enqueue the pool of items onto the free queue
end queue_manager;
```

The combination of assignments to variables at their declaration, combined with the ability to execute statements on a "once-through" basis, provides a powerful yet flexible initialisation mechanism.

6.3 PRIVATE AND LIMITED PRIVATE TYPES

In the *complex_arithmetic* example from the previous sction, we declared a record type *'complex'*, with real and inmaginary parts of type *'float'*. The programmer had complete access to the type declaration, because there was no explicit action taken in the package specification to prevent such an access. It was just another item in the visible part of the specification. There are circumstances, however, where it is desirable to declare a type for use by the outside world, but to hide the actual implementation of the type. This is achieved by making a type **private**, as in the keyboard and terminals packages, above. The effect of generating a **private** type is to remove from view all attributes of the type except its name, the predefined function for assignment, and the functions which test for equality and inequality. To illustrate, if we wished to hide the implementation details of the type "complex", we could rewrite the *complex_ arithmetic* package specification as follows:

```
package complex_arithmetic is
    type complex is private;
    function "+" (a, b : complex) return complex;
    function "-" (a, b : complex) return complex;
    function "*" (a, b : complex) return complex;
    function "/" (a, b : complex) return complex;
    function sqr (a, b : complex) return complex;
```

```
private
    type complex is
        record
            real_part   : float := 0.0;
            imag_part : float := 0.0;
        end record;
end complex_arithmetic;
```

which would then prevent a user of the package from being able to determine the structure of the type.

Let us now consider a particular problem concerning file manipulation. We wish to give a user access to any file which has a security code which matches his own, but we do not want him to be able to determine the nature of the codes themselves, since he might then be able to break them and gain access to other users' files. We can make up a package which provides a type, *'access_code'*, from which the user may generate an object (*my_code*) to hold his security code. We can then add three functions, the first of which will return to the user his own security code, the second to determine the security code for a given file and the third of which attempts to open an existing file, with the user supplying a code to be used in the attempt.

```
package file_security is
    type access_code is private;
    type    file_name is array (1. .20) of character;
    function get_my_code return access_code;
    function get_file_code (x : file_name) return access_code;
    function open_file (x : file_name;
                            y : access_code) return boolean;
private
    type access_code is integer;
end file_security;

declare
    use file_security;
    my_code : access_code;
    my_file, any_file : file_name;
begin
    . . .
    my_code := get_my_code( );
    if open_file(my_file, my_code) - - did open succeed?
    then
            - - Yes, so normal processing
    else
            - - No, so "open failure" processing
```

```
        end if;
        . . .
        if my_code = get_file_code(any_file)
                -- can I open this file for writing?
        then
                -- Yes, so process it
        else
                -- No, so give up gracefully
        end if;
    end;
```

Having declared the required objects in the declarative part of the program fragment, the user then calls the function which returns to him his access code. Note that although he now has his code, he does know what it is, nor how it is represented (it might be an integer number, a string, a pair of digits, etc.). He can now use the code in the calls to *open_file* and in the test against the value returned by *get_file_code.*

If there are circumstances where there is a need to prevent access totally to objects of a given type, except via functions expressly provided for the user, then then the use of a **limited private** type will remove the few privileges granted to **private** types (assignment and equality/inequality tests). There are some severe restrictions which apply to **limited private** types, mainly due to the absence of the assignment function. Firstly, if there is no assignment, there can be no initialisation of variables of that type when they are declared. Similarly, subprogram parameters of a limited private type cannot have default values. Lastly, constants for a limited private type cannot be declared outside the package which defines the type (how would you know they were valid if you couldn't test them, and what could you do with them?).

The **limited private** type gives the programmer the greatest degree of control over the information available to the user community. As an example, let us reconstruct the file security package:

```
    package secure_files is
        type access_code is limited private;
        type file_name is array (1. .20) of character;

        function get_my_code return access_code;
        function test_write_permission (x : file_name;
                                                y : access_code)
                                                return boolean;
        function open(x : file_name;
                        y : access_code) return boolean;
    private
        type access_code is integer;
```

```
    end secure_files;
declare
    use secure_files;
    my_code : access_code;
    any_file, my_file : file_name;
begin
    my_code := get_my_code( );
    . . .
    if open(my_file, my_code) - - did the 'open' succeed?
    then
            - - Yes, so normal processing
    else
            - - No, so "open failure" processing
    end if;
    . . .
    if test_write_permission(any_file, my_code)
            - - Can I open this file for writing?
    then
            - - Yes, so process
    else
            - - No, so give up gracefully
    end if
end;
```

In summary, packages give the programmer a powerful encapsulation mechanism, while the ability to define **private** and **limited private** types provide control over the degree of visibility of internal package structures from a user program.

CHAPTER 7

Generic Subprograms and Packages

In this chapter, we shall investigate the characteristics and uses of the generic program units; generic subprograms and generic packages.

7.1 THE GENERIC CONCEPT

There are many instances in software engineering where the programmer is required to apply the same logical function to a multiplicity of differing data objects. As an example, consider the enqueue/dequeue operations. From an overall perspective, the type of object being enqueue'd is not pertinent to the enqueue function. We might be manipulating a process to be run, a file to be printed, a character to be processed or returning a disc block to a free list. In none of these cases does the type of the object affect our understanding of the function "enqueue".

Bearing in mind the foregoing, it seems reasonable to ask whether, given the logical similarity between the operations, a means can be found to preserve this similarity when all of the various versions of "enqueue" are designed. Generic subprograms and packages are provided by Ada as a means to preserve these similarities, at the source code level. For example, the generic subprogram concept allows the programmer to design a template of an enqueue routine, from which several different instances of the enqueue subprogram may be derived at compile time, one subprogram for each kind of object to be handled.

The template of a subprogram, for instance, is given by a generic subprogram declaration and a particular instance of that template, tailored perhaps to a specific type of object, is given by a generic subprogram instantiation. It is intuitively obvious that there must be a means to pass parameters during the instantiation process in order that we may determine how to create this particular instance of the subprogram, and Ada provides the mechanisms to support such parameter passing (although with some restrictions).

In an entirely complementary manner, we can use the generic concept with packages. This gives the programmer the means to apply this new technique at a broader level of abstraction. We could envision a programmer writing a generic queue manipulation package, consisting of queue handling generic subprograms, which could be used to generate several queue handling packages, each tailored to a particular type of object.

A final point to remember is that neither a generic subprogram nor a generic package can be directly executed, only particular instances, 'instantiations', are executable.

7.2 GENERIC SUBPROGRAMS

We shall first consider the case of generic subprograms. As noted above, a generic subprogram is introduced via the generic subprogram declaration, whose syntax is:

generic_subprogram_declaration ::=
    generic_part subprogram_specification;

generic_part ::= **generic** { *generic_formal_parameter* }

generic_formal_parameter ::=
    parameter_declaration;
   | **type** *identifier* [*discriminant_part*] **is** *generic_type_definition*;
   | **with** *subprogram_specification* [**is** *name*] ;
   | **with** *subprogram_specification* **is** <>;

generic_type_definition ::=
    (<>) | **range** <> | **delta** <> | **digits** <>
   | *array_type_definition*
   | *access_type_definition*
   | *private_type_definition*

The standard example used to demonstrate the principles behind generic subprograms is the *'swap'* procedure, designed to exchange two objects of the same type. We can design a generic subprogram which will, upon instantiation, create an executable procedure capable of exchanging the contents of any two variables of the same type. The generic subprogram declaration might look like this:

    generic
        – – Define the generic parameters, a type and a subprogram
        – –
        type *object_type* **is private**;
        procedure *swap_objects* (*a, b* : **in out** *object_type*);

with a generic body as follows:

    procedure *swap_objects* (*a, b* : **in out** *object_type*) **is**
        temp : *object_type*;

```
begin
    temp := a;
      a := b;
      b := temp;
end swap_objects;
```

a generic instantiation for the enumeration type 'day':

procedure swap_day_objects **is new** swap_objects(day);

and an example of the use of the new subprogram:

```
declare
    type day is (sun, mon, tue, wed, thu, fri, sat);
    x, y : day;
begin
    . . .
    swap_day_objects(x, y);
    . . .
end;
```

Let us follow the sequence of events, all of the way from generic declaration to use of the instantiated procedure. When a generic suprogram declaration is elaborated (during the compilation process), the name of the subprogram (the subprogram identifier) is introduced and the 'generic part' is then elaborated.

Elaboration of the generic part commences with the elaboration of any generic formal parameters, in a manner similar to the elaboration of non-generic formal parameters. When all of the generic formal parameters have been elaborated, the subprogram specification is introduced. Here, there is a major difference between the actions normally taken during elaboration and those taken during the elaboration of the declaration of a generic subprogram. In the non-generic case, a subprogram specification is elaborated when it is encountered. In the elaboration of a generic subprogram's declaration, however, the subprogram specification is not elaborated at the point where it is encountered. Instead, the specification is remembered as the 'template' for the subprogram, with the elaboration actually taking place upon instantiation, when all of the substitutions of the generic actual parameters for generic formal parameters are made.

The elaboration of the body of the generic subprogram causes it to be similarly introduced as a template for future use. Like the subprogram specification, its elaboration is defered until the instantition.

We now come to the instantiation, the use of the template to create an actual instance of an executable subprogram. The syntax of the generic subprogram instantiation is:

```
generic_subprogram_instantiation ::=
    procedure identifier is generic_instantiation;
  | function designator is generic_instantiation;
```

generic_instantiation ::=
    new *name* [(*generic_association* { , *generic_association* })]

generic_association ::=
    [*formal_parameter* =>] *generic_actual_parameter*

generic_actual_parameter ::=
    expression | *subprogram_name* | *subtype_indication*

In the same way that other parameter substitutions are treated, the association between generic actual parameters and generic formal parameters can be positional, named or a default value. There is one major difference, however, in that the mode of generic parameters can only be **in** or **in out**. A parameter whose mode is **in** is treated as a constant, while one whose mode is **in out** is treated as the name of an object, equivalent to the corresponding generic actual parameter given in the instantiation. As with non-generic formal parameters, the absence of an explicit mode results in the default mode, **in,** being used.

Once the association between actual and formal parameters has been made (including the substitution of any default values), the instantiation continues with the creation of an instance of the templates and the substitution of the actual parameters for the formal ones throughout the specification and body of the new subprogram. When this is complete, the resulting instance of the subprogram is then elaborated in the usual manner. We now have a subprogram which we can use, as if we had written it by hand instead of 'automatically'.

7.3 GENERIC PACKAGES

Generic packages are very similar in concept to generic subprograms. The syntax for the generic package declaration is:

generic_package_declaration ::=
    generic_part package_specification;

with the syntax for the *generic_part* being identical to that given in the definition of the generic subprogram declaration. For generic package instantiation, the syntax is:

generic_package_instantiation ::=
    package *identifier* **is** *generic_instantiation*;

with the syntax for *generic_instantiation* again being identical to that given in section 7.2.

Let us now follow an example of the definition, instantiation, and use of a generic package which includes within it some generic subprograms. For this example, we shall address the problem of writing a generic package for implementing a circular queueing scheme, with parameters giving the length of the queue and the size of the objects to be queued. The definition of such a package might be:

```
generic
    queue_size : integer range 2. . integer'last;
    type object is private;
package queue_handler is
    procedure enqueue (a :   in object);
    procedure dequeue (a : out object);
end queue_handler;

package body queue_handler is
    subtype pointer_type is integer range 1. . queue_size + 1;
        queue    : array (1. . queue_size) of object;
      in_pointer : pointer_type := 1;
    out_pointer  : pointer_type := 1;

    procedure enqueue (a : in object) is
        begin
            if not queue_full (in_pointer, out_pointer) then
                queue (in_pointer) := a;
                in_pointer := increment (in_pointer);
            else
                put ("queue_handler, enqueue: " &
                    "You  are now out of room");
            end if;
        end enqueue;

    procedure dequeue (a : out object) is
        begin
            if not queue_empty (in_pointer, out_pointer) then
                a := queue (out_pointer);
                out_pointer := increment (out_pointer);
            else
                put ("queue_handler, dequeue:" &
                    "The queue is empty");
            end if;
        end dequeue;

    function increment (p : in pointer_type)
            return pointer_type is
        begin
            if p = queue_size then
                return (1);
            else
                return (p+1);
            end if;
```

```
        end increment_pointer;
    function queue_full (inp, outp : in pointer_type)
            return boolean is
        begin
            return ( increment(inp) = outp );
        end queue_full;

    function queue_empty (inp, outp : in pointer_type)
            return boolean is
        begin
            return (inp = outp);
        end queue_empty;
end queue_handler;
```

We can use this definition of a generic package to create two instances of the package, one of which will handle keystrokes, for example and the other disc transfer requests:

```
declare
    type key_type is new character;

    package key_queue_handler is new queue_handler
        (queue_size => 10,
            object  => key_type);
    use key_queue_handler;

    new_key, old_key : key_type;
begin
    . . .
    enqueue(new_key);
    . . .
    dequeue(old_key);
    . . .
end;

declare
    type disc_transfer_request is
        (read, write, seek, verify, format);

    package disc_transfer_handler is new queue_handler
        (queue_size => 50,
            object => disc_transfer_request);
    use disc_transfer_handler;

    next_request : disc_transfer_request;
begin
    . . .
```

find(*next_request*);
enqueue(*next_request*);
    . . .
end;

Now that we have seen some examples of how to declare, instantiate and use generic subprograms and packages, we can go back and study the details of the rules and mechanisms governing generic parameters. The first of these is the generic type definition.

7.4 GENERIC TYPE DEFINITION

The generic type definition allows the programmer to pass to the instantiation process the type of the object(s) to be manipulated within the instantiated package or subprogram. Its syntax is repeated below:

generic_type_definition ::=
    (< >) | **range** < > | **delta** < > | **digits** < >
    | *array_type_definition*
    | *access_type_definition*
    | *private_type_definition*

The "box" symbol, < >, is used in the definition of the scalar types, as follows:

(< >)	discrete types, such as enumeration, boolean and character
range < >	integer types
digits < >	floating-point types
delta < >	*fixed_point* types

with the "value" of the box being filled in upon instantiation.

The set of operations available for manipulating objects of the given type is defined by the generic formal parameter. Thus, for example, if the generic type definition includes the reserved word **digits**, the compiler knows at that point that it is dealing with a floating-point type, without having to wait until instantiation to determine the fact, and therefore knows the allowable operations for such an object. This set of operations can always be enhanced by giving a generic subprogram to perform the extra functions, as a generic formal parameter (see section 7.5), to supplement the generic type. Note that this feature is required if the programmer wishes to use the IMAGE or VALUE attributes, since these are unavailable for generic type definitions for scalar types (although the other attributes are). Some examples of generic type definitions are given below:

type *fp_type* **is digits** < >;
type *hues* **is** (< >);
type *counter* **is range** < >;
type *vector* **is array** (*counter*) **of** *fp_type*;

7.5 GENERIC FORMAL SUBPROGRAMS

The generic feature of Ada includes the ability to pass one or more subprogram specifications as part of a generic formal parameter. These "generic formal subprograms", as they are called, may themselves have parameters, although the parameter to a generic formal subprogram may not be generic. Some examples are:

> **with function** "+" (*a, b* : *complex*) **return** *complex*;
> **with procedure** *swap*(*a, b* : *item*);

A typical use of the generic formal subprogram might be the passing of a special purpose subprogram, along with a type. Thus, for example, a capital depreciation package might be passed a subprogram which computes a special depreciation schedule for objects of the corresponding type. The generic package declaration for such a package might be:

> **generic**
>   **type** *capital_object* **is** (< >);
>   **with function** *depreciation_routine*
>   (*a* : *capital_object*) **return** *float*;
> **package** *depreciation* **is**
>   . . .
> **end** *depreciation*;

The example given above is adequate, but requires that the programmer provide a subprogram for calculating the depreciation schedule for each object. What is desired is the ability to make the subprogram optional. In Ada, this is done by adding "**is** *name*" or "**is** < >" to the end of the subprogram specification. An example of the first case, a named default, is:

> **generic**
>   **type** *capital_object* **is** (< >);
>   **with function** *depreciation_routine*
>   (*a* : *capital_object*) **return** *float*
>   **is** *default_schedule;*
> **package** *depreciation* **is**
>   . . .
> **end** *depreciation*;

The use of the reserved word **is** signifies that the subprogram in whose specification it appears is an optional parameter. In the absence of a generic actual subprogram corresponding to the generic formal subprogram parameter, then the named generic formal subprogram is used. For example, given the above generic package declaration, we could use either of the following instantiations:

> - - Use a special depreciation schedule
> - -

```
package my_depreciation is new depreciation
    (        capital_object => buildings,
     depreciation_routine => inventory_depreciation);
-- Use the default depreciation schedule, default_schedule
--
package my_depreciation is new depreciation
    ( capital_object => buildings );
```

There is one further class of default generic formal subprogram, where the omission of a generic actual parameter causes the compiler to search all of the currently visible subprogram specifications to try to find one which matches in the number, order, modes and types of its parameters (and the type of the returned value and any constraints, if the formal parameter is a function). The use of "is < >" designates this type of default parameter:

```
generic
    type capital_object is (< >);
    with function depreciation_routine
                    (a : capital_object) return float
            is < >;
package depreciation is
    . . .
end depreciation;
```

which allows us to generate package instantiations such as those given below:

```
-- Use a special depreciation schedule
--
package my_depreciation is new depreciation
    (        capital_object => buildings,
     depreciation_routine => inventory_depreciation);
-- Use any depreciation schedule:
--
package my_depreciation is new depreciation
    ( capital_object => buildings );
```

7.6 MATCHING RULES FOR FORMAL AND ACTUAL PARAMETERS

The whole generic concept relies on the ability to tailor program units to a particular job, based upon the parameters passed during the instantiation process. The matching of generic formal parameters with actual parameters lies at the heart of the matter, and the remainder of this chapter is devoted to a disscussion of the rules for matching actual parameters to the formal ones.

7.6.1 Matching Scalar Types

The rules for matching a scalar type are the simplest. As mentioned in section 7.4, the appearance of $(<>)$ in a generic formal parameter will match with an actual parameter which is any enumeration type. Similarly, **range** $<>$ will match with any integer type, **digits** $<>$ with any floating-point and **delta** $<>$ with any fixed-point type. These are the only correspondences allowed.

7.6.2 Matching Array Types

For an actual array parameter to match a formal array parameter, they must both have same number of indices. This is straightforward, unless an index or the component type (or both) is a formal type. Under these circumstances, then a substitution of the actual type name for the formal type is performed, and then an attempt is made to match the actual array to the formal parameter. A match is said to occur if the types (and any constraints imposed on them) of the components are the same, corresponding index subtypes are the same, and corresponding index constraints are the same. Only if all of these conditions are met can a match be made, otherwise a CONSTRAINT_ERROR will be raised during the attempted instantiation. An example may help to clarify the rules. First, let us assume a generic package declaration of the form:

```
generic
     type item is private;
     type index is (<>);
     type unconstrained_table is array (index) of item;
     type constrained_table is array (index) range <> of item;
package example is

     . . .
end example;
```

With this declaration, we can see that a type of the form:

```
type work_hours is array (day range <>) of hours;
```

will match with the generic parameter *"constrained_table"*, but not with *"unconstrained_table"*, while the opposite is true for the type:

```
type all_hours is array (day) of hours;
```

which will only match with *"unconstrained_table"*.

7.6.3 Matching Formal Subprograms

The matching rules for formal subprograms are very similar to the rules for finding a default subprogram in section 7.5. As with packages, in the preceding section, any formal types are first substituted, before preceeding with the matching. In order for there to be a match between a formal and an actual subprogram, they must have the same number of parameters, in the same order, with the same types and modes, and with the same constraints. If the subprograms under consideration happen to be functions, then the type and constraints of the returned value must also match. Note that as in the determination for hiding (see Chapter 5, section 5.6), the parameter names and the use of default values play no part in the determination of a match. To illustrate, consider the generic subprogram specification:

> **generic**
> > **type** *item* **is private**;
> > **with function** *swap* (*a, b* : *item*) **return** *boolean* **is** <>;
> **function** *greater* (*a, b* : *item*) **return** *item*;

Given this specification, we can generate the following instances of new functions:

> **function** *bigger* **is new** *greater*(*float*);
> **function** *larger* **is new** *greater*(*character, reverse_collation*);

Note that the second instantiation requires that the function "*reverse_collation*" be visible.

7.6.4 Matching Access Types

As with the previous sections, substitutions for generic types are performed before any matching is attempted. In the case of a formal access type, an actual parameter is said to match a formal parameter if the type of the objects which are "accessed" by the access values are the same in both the formal and actual access types. As an example, given the following generic package declaration:

> **generic**
> > **type** *item* **is private**;
> > **type** *item_pointer* **is access** *item*;
> **package** *a* **is**
> > . . .
> **end** *a*;

and these types:

> **type** *queue* **is** . . .;
> **type** *queue_point* **is access** *queue*;

then we could cause an instance of the generic package to be generated like this:

> **package** *q* **is new** *a* (*item_pointer* => *queue_pointer*,
> > > > > *item* => *queue*   );

7.6.5 Matching Private Types

A private generic formal type is capable of matching any type except an unconstrained array type, subject to the constraints that if the formal type is not **limited** then the functions for assignment and testing for equality and inequality must be available, and that if the formal type has any discriminant part, then the actual type must have the same discriminants, with the same names, subtypes, and default values, and in the same order.

Note that in all of the preceding sections on matching formal types to actual ones, a CONSTRAINT_ERROR is raised by the instantiation process whenever there is a mismatch.

CHAPTER 8

Exception Handling

One of the most interesting features of Ada is the exception handling concept. The language provides built-in mechanisms which allow the programmer to specify what actions are to occur when there is an upset condition, known in Ada terminology as an "exception". This chapter is devoted to a study of the Ada approach to exceptions.

8.1 OVERVIEW

At any point during the execution of a program, there is the possibility of an error occurring. Ada defines three stages for generalised error progressing. First, there is the error itself called the "exception", secondly there is the notification that such an exception has occurred, called "raising" the exception and finally there is the action taken to cope with the exception, called "handling" the exception. As an example, consider the following program fragment:

```
declare
    x, y : float := 0.0;
begin
    . . .
    x := 1.0;
    x := x / y;    -- Note: division by zero, which would
    . . .          -- give an erroneous result.
end;
```

The exception is *caused* when we try to divide by zero. The exception is *raised* when the arithmetic processor (hardware or software, it doesn't matter which) notifies the environment of the problem, and the exception is *handled* by one of the standard system error handlers (NUMERIC-ERROR, in this case) which might print an error message and then terminate the program.

In most other languages which are widely available, such as Fortran, Basic, Cobol, etc., the detection of the error is the responsibility of the software and/or hardware environment in which the program is running. Similarly, the actions taken in response to the error are usually beyond the user's control. If the above fragment were to have been written in Fortran, for example, there is no mechanism which would allow the programmer to specify that he was aware that his program might try to divide by zero and that he wished for some special code to be executed if this happened, instead of the program being aborted. His only recourse is to laboriously test all variables before using them, throughout his program.

The Ada solution to these problems is to allow the programmer to declare an exception (giving it a name), to give him the means to raise the exception and allow him to provide an exception handler which can be executed in response to the raising of the exception.

8.2 EXCEPTION DECLARATION

The purpose of the exception declaration is to introduce the name of an exception, which can then be used in exception handlers and **raise** statements (see Chatper 2, section 2.6). The syntax of the exception declaration is:

exception declaration ::= *identifier_list* : **exception**;

Using the division-by-zero example above, we could write a subprogram in such a way as to allow us to raise that exception ourselves:

```
function percent (a, b : integer) return float is
    zero_divide : exception;
begin
    if b = 0 then
        raise zero_divide;
    else
        return ( float(a)/float(b)*100.0 );
    end if;
end percent;
```

Note that the general concept of declaring an entity (the exception) before its use (in the **raise** statement) has been followed, but that we have not yet specified where the exception handler is, nor what effect it has.

Note also that the language provides the following pre-defined exceptions:

CONSTRAINT_ERROR	Raised when a range, index or discriminat constraint is violated.
NUMERIC_ERROR	Raised when a predefined numeric operation gives a result which does not lie within the implemented range of the target object.
SELECT_ERROR	Raised all the alternatives of a **select** statement are closed *and* it has no **else** part.

STORAGE_ERROR   Raised if there is insufficient storage to satisfy
                         the execution of an allocator or if a task runs
                         out of dynamic storage.
TASKING_ERROR   Raised if an exception occurs during inter-task
                         communication.

which therefore do not need to be declared.

8.3 THE RAISE STATEMENT

The **raise** statement is used to indicate that the programmer wishes to explicitly
raise an exception (we have already met the **raise** statement in Chapter 2, section
2.6). Its syntax is as follows:

  raise_statement ::= **raise** [*exception_name*] ;

From this syntax definition, it can be seen that the exception name is optional.
Although it cannot be determined from the syntax, omission of the exception
name is only allowed if the **raise** statement is within an exception handler.
Under these circumstances, the effect is that the exception which caused the
entry to the handler is raised again.

8.4 THE EXCEPTION HANDLER

The exception handler provides the linkage between the exception named in the
raise statement (or one of the predefined exceptions) and the actual statements
which will be executed in response to the raising of the exception. It can only
appear at the end of a block or at the end of the body of a subprogram, package
or task, its syntax being:

  exception_handler ::=
      when *exception_choice* { | *exception_choice* }=>
          sequence_of_statements
  exception_choice ::= *exception_name* | **others**

We have already seen examples of where an exception handler may be located,
in the syntactical definition of the subprogram body (see Chapter 5, section 5.2),
for example.

In order to explore the sequence of events which takes place when an
exception is raised and then handled, let us return to our divide-by-zero example,
this time providing our own exception handler:

```
function percent (a, b : integer) return float is
    zero_divide : exception;
begin
    if b = 0 then
        raise zero_divide;
    else
        return ( float(a)/float(b)*100.0 );
    end if;
```

```
    exception
        when zero_divide =>
            put("percent: Attempt to divide by zero");
            return 0.0;
    end percent;
```

We are now in a position to be able to completely handle the divide-by-zero case ourselves. When the divide-by-zero condition is detected ($y=0$), we raise the "*zero_divide*" exception. Raising the exception causes execution of the unit (block, subprogram body, package body, or task body) to be suspended and a search is performed to determine whether there is a handler specified by the programmer for this exception. If there is, execution continues with the named handler, otherwise execution of the unit is terminated and the exception will be "propagated" forward (see section 8.5). In our example, we find that there is an exception handler for *zero_divide,* so execution therefore continues with the "put" statement in the exception handler. Note that any statements which occur between the **raise** statement and the exception handler are skipped.

There are two important points to note about this example. Firstly, execution of the subprogram has not been abandoned when the exception handler is entered, it is merely a transfer of control. This is important, especially when the exception occurs in a main program or task, since the absence of a user-supplied handler would result in the termination of the program or task. If an exception handler has been supplied, then the user retains control over whether the program terminates. Secondly, because the exception handler is a part of the unit, it has access to all of the unit's resources. Thus, in the example above, we can perform a **return** statement for the function. Similarly, there may be an opportunity to perform some corrective actions before retrying the original operation (being careful to avoid infinite loops and deadly embraces, of course).

If we had to test for division by zero all over the place, we would not be significantly better off than the poor Fortran programmer above. We can, however, specify an exception handler for the predefined exceptions, which allows us to rewrite the example as follows:

```
    function percent (a, b : integer) return float is
    begin
        return ( float(a)/float(b)*100.0 );
    exception
        when NUMERIC_ERROR =>
            if b = 0 then
                put("percent: Attempt to divide by zero");
            else
                put("percent: NUMERIC_ERROR");
            end if;
            return 0.0;
    end percent;
```

If "b" happens to be zero, the predefined NUMERIC_ERROR exception will be raised in the normal course of events. In this example, however, we have supplied our own exception handler to catch this error, which allows us to perform the **return** and continue with the calling program. Note that there is no explicit testing or raising of the exception for the programmer to perform, it is all handled automatically. Note also the extra code in the exception handler which determines whether the exception was actually caused by division by zero, since we cannot know for certain what caused the NUMERIC_ERROR and it might have been something else in our calculations.

Finally, there is nothing to prevent us from explicitly raising a predefined exception. We could have written the divide-by-zero example to use NUMERIC_ ERROR:

```
function percent (a, b : integer) return float is
begin
     if b = 0 then
          raise NUMERIC_ERROR;
     else
          return ( float(a)/float(b)*100.0 );
     end if;
exception
     when NUMERIC_ERROR =>
          put("percent: Attempt to divide by zero");
          return 0.0;
end percent;
```

which would have had the same effect as the example in which we declared and used the "*zero_divide*" exception.

There is one final construct which remains to be explored, namely the **others** clause of the exception handler. It can be used as a "safety net" to catch all exceptions which have no explicit handler, as in this case:

```
function percent (a, b : integer) return float is
begin
     return ( float(a)/float(b)*100.0 );
exception
     when NUMERIC_ERROR =>
          put("percent: NUMERIC_ERROR");
          return 0.0;
     when others =>
          put("percent: Unknown Exception");
          return 0.0;
end percent;
```

8.5 LINKING EXCEPTIONS TO HANDLERS

We now turn to a study of the mechanisms used to search for a handler to handle an exception, once it has been raised, and the rules governing the propogation of an exception and the rules for termination of a unit. These form the heart of the Ada exception handling system.

There are two classes of rules to be studied, those for exceptions raised during the elaboration of declarations and those raised during the execution of statements. It is convenient to investigate them separately.

8.5.1 Exceptions Raised During Elaborations

The action taken when an exception occurs during an elaboration depends upon what is being elaborated. Let us take, for example, a subprogram the elaboration of whose declaration can cause an exception to be raised:

```
function search (a : character;
                 b : string      ) return integer;
     index : integer := b'last+1;      -- beyond end of string
     char : character := b(index);     -- a constraint error
begin
     . . .
end search;
```

If an exception is raised during the elaboration of the declarative part of a subprogram, as it is here, then the elaboration is abandoned and the exception is raised in the unit which caused the elaboration. To illustrate, let us use the above example in a larger setting:

```
declare
     start : integer := search('i', "Hi There");
begin
     . . .
end;
```

If we wished to handle the CONSTRAINT_ERROR which is raised in the elaboration of the declarative part of *"search"*, we should have to provide it in the block, *not* in the subprogram. Thus, we would have to write something like this:

```
declare
     function search (a : character;
                      b : string      ) return integer;
          index : integer := b'last+1;       -- beyond end of string
          char  : character := b(index);     -- a constraint error
                                             -- will be generated
                                             -- when this is elaborated.
```

```
begin
     . . .
end search;
declare
     start : integer;
begin
     . . .
     start := search('i', "Hi There");
     . . .
exception
     when CONSTRAINT_ERROR =>
          block_handler;
end;
end;
```

We can thus state the propagation rules for an exception raised during the elaboration of the declarative part of a subprogram as being that the exception will cause the elaboration of the declarative part to be abandoned and the exception raised in the calling unit, unless the subprogram is the main program, in which case execution of the program is terminated. It is therefore the responsibility of the calling unit to provide the necessary exception handlers, if it wishes to.

The rules for an exception which is raised in the declarative part of a block are very similar. The elaboration of the declarative part is abandoned, and the exception carried to the unit which includes the block. This is illustrated in the example below. Compare this to the previous example, noting that in this case the exception is handled by "something_handler", not "block_handler".

```
procedure something is;
     function search (a : character;
                      b : string      ) return integer;
          index : integer := b'last+1 ;
          char  : character := b(index);
     begin
          . . .
     end search;
begin
     declare
          start : integer := search('i', "Hi There");
     begin
          . . .
     exception
          when CONSTRAINT_ERROR =>
               block_handler;
     end;
```

```
exception
    when CONSTRAINT_ERROR =>
        something_handler;
end something;
```

For an exception raised during the elaboration of the declarative part of a package body, the elaboration is again abandoned and the exception propogated to the unit containing the body. If the package happens to be a library unit, then the program is abandoned.

If an exception is raised during the elaboration of the declarative part of a task body, then the elaboration is abandoned and the exception propagated to the unit which caused the task to be activated.

If the exception occurs during the elaboration of a subprogram declaration, package declaration or task declaration (as opposed to an exception raised during the elaboration of a declarative part), then the elaboration is abandoned and the exception propagated to the unit containing the declaration. As before, if subprogram declaration or package declaration is the declaration of a library unit, then the program is terminated.

8.5.2 Exceptions Raised During Statement Execution

The precise sequence of events which takes place when an exception occurs during the execution of a statement is dependent on the unit which encloses the statement in question. We have already gained an intuitive feel for the process during our discussions on the syntactical side of exceptions and exception handlers (sections 8.1 to 8.4). It is now time to provide a little more detail.

If an exception is raised during the execution of a block which has not provided a handler for that exception, then execution of the block is terminated and the same exception is raised in the unit which contains the block. This can be illustrated as follows:

```
outer:
declare
    . . .
begin
    . . .
    inner:
    declare
        type small_int is range 0..10;
        a : small_int;
    begin
        . . .
        a := 10;
        a := a * a; - - CONSTRAINT_ERROR raised here
        . . .
```

```
        end inner;
          . . .
    exception
        when CONSTRAINT_ERROR =>
                    . . .
    end outer;
```

The CONSTRAINT_ERROR raised in the block "*inner*" causes the remainder of the statements in "*inner*" to be skipped and the exception to be raised again in "*outer*". Since "*outer*" has an exception handler for that particular exception, execution continues with that handler.

The next case to examine is that of an exception raised by the execution of a statement in a subprogram body which has not provided an appropriate exception handler. Under these circumstances, execution of the subprogram is abandoned and the same exception raised again at the point of call (unless this is the main program, in which case the program is terminated).

```
    declare
        procedure xyz;  - - Always raises NUMERIC_ERROR
        begin
            . . .
        end;
        procedure abc;  - - Always raises CONSTRAINT_ERROR
        begin
            . . .
        end;
    begin
        . . .
        xyz:  - - Handled by outer_handler
        . . .
        declare
            . . .
        begin
            . . .
            abc;  - - Handled by general_handler
            . . .
            xyz;  - - Handled by inner_handler
            . . .
        exception
            when NUMERIC_ERROR =>
                    inner_handler;
        end;
        . . .
```

```
exception
    when NUMERIC_ERROR =>
        outer_handler;
    when others =>
        general_handler;
end;
```

If we now look at an exception raised in a package body, we find that in the absence of a handler provided in the package, elaboration of the package is abandoned (remember, elaboration of a package consists of elaboration of its declarative part, followed by execution of any statements, so it is correct to say that the elaboration is abandoned) and the exception is raised again in the unit which contains the package body. As in section 8.5.1, if the package is a library unit, the main program is terminated.

For an exception raised during the execution of a task body and for which there is no handler, the task is terminated. There is no propagation of the exception.

The last case we have to deal with is that of the execution of a statement in an exception handler causing a further exception. If this occurs, execution of the unit is abandoned and the exception is propagated as above.

8.5.3 Exceptions Raised During Task Communications

The synchronisation and communication primatives provided in Ada to support tasking are the **entry** and **accept** statements (see Chapter 9, on 'Tasking', for details). A task issues an **entry** call to another task (which is executing asynchronously with the calling task) while the called task issues an **accept** statement where it will wait for the **entry** call before executing the statements associated with the **accept**. This can result in an exception being raised in one of two ways. Firstly, the called task may have been terminated and cannot therefore have issued an **accept** statement. This situation will result in the TASKING_ERROR exception being raised in the calling task at the point of the call, as below:

```
task body a is
    . . .
begin
    . . .
    x . read(char);  -- Raises TASKING_ERROR, as task x defunct
    . . .
exception
    when TASKING_ERROR =>
        . . .
end a;
```

Note that this form of exception can only affect the calling task, since the called task is not executing.

The second form of exception which can occur is when the execution of the statements associated with the called task's **accept** statement cause an exception for which there is not a local handler (local meaning within the unit containing the **accept**). If this happens, then the exception is propogated according to the rules given in section 8.5.2 and also propagated back to the calling task, at the point of the call.

There is one futher exception which concerns tasks, and that is the FAILURE attribute. Tasks are types, and as such they have attributes, among which is the attribute FAILURE. Ada allows any task to raise this exception in another task by writing:

raise *his*'FAILURE;

where "*his*" is the name of the task in which the exception is to be raised. This has no effect on the task which issues the **raise**, but has the effect of "interrupting" the target task ("*his*"). If the target task was suspended, it is awoken so that it may cope with the upset.

8.6 SUPPRESSION OF CHECKING

In order for the predefined exceptions to be raised, it is reasonable to assume that there are checks which are applied to determine whether to raise the corresponding exception (e.g. checking on array bounds). Ada allows the programmer to selectively "turn off" these checks, by means of a **pragma** whose syntax is:

pragma SUPPRESS (*check_name* [, [ON =>] *name*]);

This allows the programmer to suppress a particular check (within a block or the body of a subprogram, package or task), optionally on a particular type. The following examples should help to illustrate the point:

pragma SUPPRESS (OVERFLOW_CHECK);
pragma SUPPRESS (INDEX_CHECK ON => *vector*);

The checks which are performed, and which may thus be turned off are:

ACCESS_CHECK	Check for a **null** access value when attempting to use an access value to access an object.
DISCRIMINANT_CHECK	Check that a record component exists and satisfies any discriminant constraints.
INDEX_CHECK	Check an index value satisfies any constraints or it compatible with an index type.
LENGTH_CHECK	Check there are the required number of components for an index.

RANGE_CHECK	Check that a value satisfies a range constraint or that a constraint is compatible with a type mark.
DIVISION_CHECK	Check for division by zero.
OVERFLOW_CHECK	Check a numeric result for overflow.
STORAGE_CHECK	Check for sufficient space.

Note that the STORAGE_ERROR is generated by the STORAGE_CHECK, NUMERIC_ERROR by DIVISION_CHECK or OVERFLOW_CHECK and that CONSTRAINT_ERROR is generated by the others.

As a final word on suppression of checking, it is important to remember that the SUPPRESS pragma is only a recommendation to the compiler that it may leave out the corresponding run-time checks. There is still the possibility that an exception will occur, due to the propagation rules. In general, unless there are *very* strong reasons to do otherwise, checking should never be suppressed. It is a safeguard which should not be thrown away lightly.

CHAPTER 9

Tasking

In this chapter, we shall cover the Ada constructs which support the generation and maintenance of tasks (sometimes known in other languages as processes) as well as the task synchronisation and communication mechanisms.

9.1 OVERVIEW
A task in Ada may be thought of as a program unit which can execute independently in time from other tasks. This asynchronous operation requires that cooperating tasks have constructs available which support synchronisation and communication between them. As an example, let us consider the problem of writing a line-numbering task, or spooler, whose function is to accept data from a user task, add line numbers and pagination, and hand the transformed data on to a second task, the printer driver. This requires that the user task be able to send messages to the line-numbering task, that the line-numbering task be capable of waiting until such time as it receives the data and that the line-numbering task be able to send messages to the driver task. The specification for the line-numbering task might be:

```
task line_numberer is
    entry get_data(a : in item);
end x;
```

and the corresponding task body like this:

```
task body line_numberer is
    temp : item:
begin
    loop
        accept get_data(a : in item) do
            temp := transform(m);
            printer_driver . put_data(temp);
        end;
    end loop;
end x;
```

There are several points to notice about the example. First, as with other Ada objects, there is a specification and a corresponding body. Second, the specification defines the interface between this task and any cooperating tasks which wish to interect with it, via the **entry** statement. Finally, note that printer task would have an **entry** statement defining the code for *put_data,* as *"line_numberer"* has for *get_data.*

It is important to understand that we have nowhere specified any requirements about *when* any of the tasks should run, nor how fast. They are independent and can execute in parallel, perhaps even on different machines. The only things we know with certainty are that *"line_numberer"* will wait for input from a user task and will send its output to the printer task (which will presumably be waiting for output from *"line_numberer"*). Even this description is somewhat erroneous, since if the line-numbering task produces output faster than the printer task can handle it, the excess will be queue'd (within reason). In this fashion the time dependencies are minimised.

Having gained a flavour for tasking, let us now turn our attention to the definition of a task and examine it in more detail.

9.2 TASK DEFINITION

As with subprograms and packages, tasks must be declared before they can be used and are defined in terms of a task specification and a task body. The syntax for the task declaration is:

task_declaration ::= *task_specification*

task_specification ::=
    task [**type**] *identifier* [**is**
        { *entry_declaration* }
        { *representation_specification* }
    end [*identifier*]];

task_body ::=
    task body *identifier* **is**
        [*declarative_part*]
    begin
        sequence_of_statements
    [**exception**
        { *exception_handler* }]
    end [*identifier*];

The task specification defines the interface between the task and the remainder of the system. It performs the same sort of function as the subprogram specification (see Chapter 5, section 5.2). It sets forth the "entry points" to the task, those identifiers which are visible to the system and which can be called by other tasks. In addition, the task specification may include a representation specification for a particular type, giving information about such items as the amount of storage the task requires and machine dependencies such as the physical address of a peripheral.

As with other specification-body pairs, the identifiers for the body and the specification must match each other and also the optional identifier after the final **ends**. There is an additional restriction with task specifications that the specification must appear in the same declarative part as the task body, and must appear before it in the text.

A task in Ada is an object, and as with other Ada objects, a task object has a type associated with it, defined by the task specification. Once a task type has been defined, it may be used to generate corresponding task objects. For example, suppose that in the line-numbering example there had been several printers to choose from. There would have to be several printer tasks to drive them, each different from the others but each performing the same functions. We could define a task type *"printer_driver"* as follows:

```
task type printer_driver is
    entry put_data(a : item);
    entry reset;
end printer_driver;
task body printer_driver is
    . . .
begin
    . . .
end printer_driver;
```

With the above task type defined, we could then use it to declare the required printer driver tasks:

```
declare
    printer_1, printer_2, printer_3 : printer_driver;
    x : item;
    . . .
begin
    printer_2 . reset;
    . . .
    printer_2 . put_data(x);
    . . .
end;
```

Here, we have declared three task objects, using one of them, *"printer_2"* to illustrate their use. In particular, note that in order to specify the particular task's entry we wish to access, we have to use component selection.

Note that a task type defines the set of entries possessed by corresponding task objects. In addition, note that since tasks are objects, they can be used in arrays or records, subject to the restriction that there is no assignment or equality-inequality testing available for task objects (in this respect, task objects can be thought of as being generated from a **limited private** type, with the value of the objects being defined on elaboration of the object declaration or on its creation via an allocator). It follows from the above that a task object cannot be used as a actual parameter when the formal parameter has a mode of **in out** or **out**. The passing of a task object is allowed, however, if the mode is **in**.

As a final note, if you look back at the syntax definition of the task specification, you will see that the word **type** is optional. If omitted, the specification and corresponding body introduce a single task object, known by the given identifier, rather than introducing a task type and thereafter requiring explicit object declarations.

9.3 TASK ATTRIBUTES

Task types and task objects, in keeping with other Ada types and objects have attributes associated with them. The values of these attributes may be determined by using the following attribute enquiry functions on a task object or type ("a", for example):

a'PRIORITY The priority of the task "a", if it is defined. Its value is an integer of the subtype PRIORITY (see section 9.10).

a'STORAGE_SIZE The number of units of storage allocated to the task "a", an integer.

a'TERMINATED A boolean value, set to false when the task "a" is declared and to true when "a" is terminated (see section 9.5).

In addition to the attributes associated with the task itself, there is an additional enquiry function, COUNT, which allows the programmer to determine the number of entry calls on the queue for a particular entry, "a", for example:

a'COUNT An integer count of the number of entry calls in the queue associated with the entry "a".

9.4 TASK GENERATION AND INITIATION

We have discussed the syntax of task definition, but have yet to elaborate on the sequence of events which occurs when a task object is declared, nor have we said precisely when a task starts to execute.

As with other declarations, a task object is declared during the elaboration of the declarative part of a unit. With tasks, however, there is an additional step beyond merely introducing the object itself. The execution of a task is started in response to its "activation", which consists of elaborating the task body's declarative part after which the sequence of statements which make up the remainder of the task body are executed. Note that this means that the task will be executing *before* any statements which follow the declarative part of the unit in which it is declared. To illustrate:

> **declare**
>
> . . .
>
> *printer*_1 : *printer_driver*; - - *printer*_1 elaborated
>
> . . .
>
> **begin**
>
> - - *printer*_1 activated, executing by this point.
> *First_statement*;
>
> . . .
>
> **end**;

When more than one task is declared in the same declarative part, the order in which they are activated is undefined:

> **declare**
>
> . . .
>
> *printer*_1, *printer*_2 : *printer_driver*;
> *printer*_3 : *printer_driver*,
>
> . . .
>
> **begin**
>
> - - *printer*_1, _2, _3 activated in undefined sequence!
> . . .
>
> **end**;

If a task object is generated by an allocator, it is activated and starts executing. Execution of the allocator is not complete until the task has been activated. This means that we now have some control over the order of activation of tasks. Thus, we have the following:

> **declare**
>
> . . .
>
> **type** *dynamic_printer* **is access** *printer_driver*;
> *printer*_1, *printer*_2 : *printer_driver*;
> *spare_printer* : *dynamic_printer* := **new** *printer_driver*;
> - - *spare_printer* activated here! !
>
> . . .
>
> **begin**
>
> - - *printer*_1, _2 activated here, all three tasks now
> - - executing.
>
> . . .
>
> **end**;

Note that a task's entry can be called even if the task has not yet been activated, since the entry calls are queued up for processing.

We now have to deal with the possibility of an exception being raised during the activation of a task. There are really only four rules to follow when an exception occurs:

1. Any previously activated tasks are unaffected.
2. Any subsequent tasks are deemed "terminated" (see below).
3. The exception is treated as if it occured in the statements following the declarative part.
4. If the execption occurrs in the declarative part itself, all tasks elaborated so far are terminated.

The next two examples should clarify the rules stated above:

declare
      p_1, p_2 : *printer_driver*;
      spare : *printer_driver*; - - exception caused here
      p_3 : *printer_driver*;
begin
      - - *p_1, p_2* executing, *spare* and *p_3* terminated.
      . . .
end;
declare
      p_1, p_2 : *printer_driver*;
      x : *integer* **range** $1..10 := y$; - - causes exception
      spare : *printer_driver*;
      p_3 : *printer_driver*;
begin
      - - *p_1, p_2, p_3* and *spare* all terminated.
      . . .
end;

9.5 TASK TERMINATION

Now that we have a running task, it is time to see how it is stopped, or "terminated".

As has been stated above, a task is declared in the declarative part of a block, subprogram, etc. Take the following example:

declare
      . . .
      p_1 : *printer_driver*;
      . . .
begin
      - - *p_1* activated here
      . . .
end;

Looking at the above example, it seems reasonable to ask what happens to both the task and the block (the unit declaring the task) when the end of the block is reached? To answer this point we need to introduce the concept of "task dependency". In Ada, each task "depends" on a block, subprogram body, task body or library package. In other words, for a given unit, a task is said to be a "dependent" task if it is declared within the unit (including an inner package) but not within an inner unit, or if the task is designated by the value of an access type and the access type was declared within the unit (including an inner package) and not within a inner unit.

We can now provide an answer to the question posed at the top of the previous paragraph. The language definition specifies that a unit (the block in our case) is not left until all dependent tasks have terminated. Thus, the task "p_1" must terminate before we can exit from the block. Note that this rule applies even in the case of an exception for which there is no exception handler, which would attempt to force an exit.

From the point of view of the task, it terminates when the end of the task body is reached and when all of it's dependent tasks (if any) have terminated. A task may also terminate as a result of executing a **terminate** in a select statement (see below). The example demonstrates the dependencies:

```
task type timer is . . . end timer;

declare
    . . .
    type at_timer is access timer;
    a : timer;
    . . .
begin
    - - "a" activated here.
    . . .
    declare
        . . .
        b : timer;
        c : at_timer := new timer;
        - - "c . all" activated here
        . . .
    begin
        - - "b" activated here
        . . .
    end; - - Wait here for termination of "b"
    . . .
end;      - - Wait here for termination of "a" and "c . all"
```

9.6 THE RENDEZVOUS CONCEPT

In order for two tasks to synchronise themselves both tasks must agree to "meet", with the earlier arrival waiting for the later one. This is the "rendezvous" concept, implemented in Ada with the **entry** and **accept** statements, and whose syntax definition is as follows:

entry_declaration ::=
    entry *identifier* [(*discrete_range*)] [*formal_part*] ;

entry_call ::= *entry_name* [*actual_parameter_part*] ;

accept_statement ::=
    accept *entry_name* [*formal_part*] **do**
        sequence_of_statements
    end [*identifier*] ;

A task's **entry** declarations define the interface of the task to the rest of the system. For each **entry** declaration in the task specification there is a corresponding **accept** statement in the task body. There may in fact be more than one **accept** statement for a particular **entry,** in which case the calling task must use an index to completely specify the call it wishes to make. To illustrate, with a task specification and body as follows:

```
task type printer_driver is
    entry write(speed) (a : item);
end printer_driver;

task body printer_driver is
    . . .
begin
    . . .
    accept write(slow) (a : item) do
        . . .
    end;
    . . .
    accept write(fast) (a : item) do
        . . .
    end;
    . . .
end printer_driver;
```

the calling task would have to use the following to access the entry *"write"*:

```
declare
    a : printer_driver;
    x, y : item;
```

```
begin
    . . .
    a . write(slow) (x);
    a . write(fast) (y);
    . . .
end;
```

In cases like this, where there are a series of **accept** statements for a single **entry,** there is said to be an entry "family". Since indexing is used to uniquely determine the required **accept** statement from within the family, there is the possibility that the exception CONSTRAINT_ERROR will be raised if the index range is violated.

We now come to the heart of the rendezvous system, a discussion of the sequence of events leading up to the execution of the sequence of statements associated with an **accept** statement. When an entry is called, the calling task is suspended until the statements associated with the **accept** (if there are any) have been executed. There are now two possibilities; the called task is already waiting at the **accept** statement, in which case the sequence of statements may be executed immediately, or there may be an undefined interval of time required for the called task to reach the **accept.** In either case, by making the calling task wait until the execution of the sequence of statements associated with the **accept** has been completed, we have effectively synchronised the two tasks. This is the Ada "rendezvous", and once the statements linked to the **accept** have executed, both the calling and the called task are free to execute in parallel. The next example demonstrates the principles we have just discussed:

```
task a is
    entry sync;
end a;
task body a is
begin
    loop
        . . .
        accept sync do
            null;
        end sync;
        . . .
    end loop;
end a;
declare
    . . .
begin
    . . .
    a . sync;
```

next;   - - Executed after the "**end** *sync*;" of the task
                         - - "*a*".

    . . .

  end;

In the previous paragraphs, it was stated that it was possible to call an entry before the called task was even activated. This is possible because each **entry** has a single queue associated with it. As entries are called, they are placed into the queue. The called task then unqueues them, one at a time, each time the corresponding **accept** statement is executed. Note that it is defined in the Ada language that the queue is processed on a "first-in, first-out" basis. As stated before, any attempt to call an entry in a task which has terminated will result in the exception TASKING_ERROR.

9.7 THE DELAY STATEMENT

There are many instances in programming, especially in operating systems programming, where it is desirable to be able to have a task suspend execution for a period of time. In order to complement fully the tasking concepts of Ada, the **delay** statement has been made a part of the language to provide this function. Its syntax is:

delay_statement ::= **delay** *simple_expression*;

The simple expression, which is interpreted as a time delay in seconds, must evaluate to conform with the constraints imposed by the implementation dependent, predefined, fixed-point type DURATION, found in the package STANDARD. The language definition, however, requires that it be able to represent values up to 86400, which is the number of seconds in a day. A use of the **delay** statement might be as follows:

```
declare
    tick : constant DURATION := 1.0; - - Interval in secs.
    counter : integer := 0;
begin
    loop
        delay tick; - - Wait for about one second
        counter := counter + 1;
    end loop;
end;
```

It is very important to understand that the **delay** statement does *not* guarantee a delay of exactly the specified time, only that the delay will be at least that long. It is very possible that the actual delay will be longer, due to such factors as system loading, task scheduling delays, etc.

Use of the **delay** statement with a negative argument is logically meaningless, and has no effect on the task executing the statement.

9.8 THE SELECT STATEMENT

It is implicit in the execution of an **entry** call that the calling task is prepared to cease execution for an undetermined period of time. Even worse, in cases where the possibility of a delay is unacceptable, the calling program may not have direct access to the parameters which would allow it to perform its own tests, prior to making the call. The same is true for the **accept** statement. The **select** statement is designed to address some of these problems, by providing the programmer with some measure of control over whether to execute an **accept** or **entry** call. The syntax of the **select** statement is as follows:

select_statement ::=
    selective_wait
  | *conditional_entry_call*
  | *timed_entry_call*

9.8.1 Conditional Entry Calls

The conditional entry call is used in cases where the programmer wishes to test whether it is possible for the rendezvous with the called task to place immediately. Its syntax is:

conditional_entry_call ::=
    select
        entry_call [*sequence_of_statements*]
    else
        sequence_of_statements
    end select;

If the calling task cannot immediately rendezvous with the called task, then the statements associated with the **else** part are executed. If the rendezvous can be satisfied immediately, then the **entry** call is issued. To illustrate, consider the problem of a task which must poll a keyboard to see if a key is depressed and when it finds one to place it in a queue. If it cannot queue up a key for processing, it must set a flag for some other task in the system. Our task might look like this:

    task *keyboard* **is**
        entry *reset*;
    end *keyboard*;
    task body *keyboard* **is**
        . . .
        flag : *boolean* := *false*;
        key : *character*;
        . . .

```
begin
    loop
        read_keys(key);
        select
                a . queue(key);
                flag := false;
        else
                flag := true;
        end select;
    end loop;
end keyboard;
```

9.8.2 Timed Entry Calls

The timed entry call is similar to the conditional entry call, except that in this case, the test performed is not to determine whether the rendezvous can be satisfied immediately, but whether it can be satisfied within a given period of time. The syntax of the timed entry call is:

```
timed_entry_call ::=
    select
            entry_call [sequence_of_statements]
    or
            delay_statement [sequence_of_statements]
    end select;
```

With the timed entry call, the named entry is only called if the rendezvous can be started within the amount of time specified in the delay statement, otherwise the delay statement is executed. Let us again illustrate with the example of a keyboard task, except that this time, if we cannot queue up a key, we will wait, and after three tries, give up:

```
task keyboard is
    entry reset;
end keyboard;
task body keyboard is
    . . .
    counter : integer := 0;
    limit : constant integer := 3;
    flag : boolean := false;
    key : character;
    . . .
```

```
begin
    loop
        read_keys(key);
        select
            a . queue(key);
            counter := 0;  -- Reset counter if successful!
        or
            delay 0.5;
            counter := counter + 1:
        end select;
        exit when counter > 3;
    end loop;
end keyboard;
```

9.8.3 The Selective Wait Statement

We now turn to the last of the select statements, the selective wait. The preceding sections dealt with the options available to the user of the **entry** statement and the selective wait statement complements them by providing control over the **accept** statement. The syntax for the selective wait statement is:

```
selective_wait ::=
    select
    [when condition =>]
        selective_alternative
    { or [when condition =>]
        selective_alternative }
    [else
        sequence_of_statements]
    end select;
selective_alternative ::=
    accept_statement [sequence_of_statements]
    | delay_statement [sequence_of_statements]
    | terminate;
```

The following example shows a possible use of the selective wait statement:

```
task body space_manager is
    . . .
begin
    loop
        . . .
        select
            when space_available =>
                accept allocate_space do
                    . . .
                end;
```

```
              or
                accept return_space do

                     . . .

                end;
              end select;
          end loop;
     end space_manager;
```

When the select statement is executed, a test is made to determine which of the select alternatives are "*open*", that is those alternatives which either have no **when** clause, or whose **when** clauses evaluate to "*true*". The choice of which of the open alternatives to execute then depends upon the alternatives themselves, as follows:

delay   If any open alternative starts with a **delay** statement, then the delay value is evaluated immediately after the **when** conditions are evaluated. The **delay** alternative will be selected if none of the other alternatives have been selected before the specified delay time has elapsed.

accept   If an open alternative starts with an **accept** statement, then it *may* be selected if another task has issued an entry call for this accept (see below). If this alternative is selected, then the **accept** statement and any corresponding sequence of statements are executed.

terminate   If an open alternative uses the **terminate** statement, then it may only be selected if this task is dependent on a unit and the end of that unit has been reached (it is awaiting the termination of its dependent tasks). In addition, this alternative may only be selected if all other dependent tasks of the unit are either terminated or waiting at a **terminate** alternative. Note that if the unit on which this task is dependent is itself a task, then the definition of the end includes a **terminate** alternative. Execution of a terminate statement causes a task to terminate normally.

If none of the alternatives can be immediately selected, then if an **else** part exists it is executed, otherwise the task will wait until an open alternative can be selected. If none of the alternatives are open, then if an **else** part exists it will be executed, otherwise the exception SELECT_ERROR will be raised. The next few examples should clarify these rules:

```
     . . .
     open := true;
```

```
select
    when open =>
        accept xyz do
            . . .
        end;
or
    when not open =>
        accept abc do
            . . .
        end;
end select;
```

In this example, the first alternative is open (because the condition is true) whereas the second is not. If another task has made an entry call to "*xyz*", then the **accept**, being the only open alternative, will be selected. If no such entry call has been issued, then the task will wait for it, since there is no **else** part to be executed.

```
. . .
open := true;
select
    when open =>
        accept xyz do
            . . .
        end;
or
    accept abc do
        . . .
    end;
end select;
```

In this example, both alternatives are open. If no entry calls for either "*abc*" or "*xyz*" have been issued then the task will wait for the first one. If, however, an entry call has been issued for both, then *the choice of alternatives is made arbitrarily*. This is why the description of the **accept** alternative above specified only that an open alternative *may* be chosen. Given that there are several accept alternatives, all of which are open and which can immediately perform a rendezvous, there are no guarantees as to which alternative will actually be chosen.

9.9 ABORTING TASKS

The **abort** statement is a means of abnormally terminating one or more tasks. Its syntax is:

abort_statement ::= **abort** *task_name* { , *task_name* };

Because the termination is abnormal, not only is the named task terminated, but so are any tasks which are dependent on it or any units called by it. As you would expect, if the named task has yet to be activated, it is terminated, and if it is already terminated there is no effect. In terms of the effect of the execution an **abort** statement on a rendezvous, the following rules are applied:

1. If the task being aborted is in the process of calling an entry, then the entry call is removed from the called task's queue.
2. If the task being aborted is already in the process of executing a rendezvous, then the calling task is aborted and the called task is allowed to complete its **accept** normally.
3. If the task aborted has any outstanding entries, then the TASKING_ ERROR exception is raised in all of the tasks which issued the entry calls, at the point of the call. If the call was a timed entry call, the delay is cancelled.

This method of abnormally terminating tasks is designed as a last resort, for cases where everything else has failed. The recommended means of terminating a task is to raise the FAILURE exception in the task, which allows the task being terminated the option of tidying up before terminating, by executing an exception handler for FAILURE. The **abort** statement does not allow even that.

9.10 TASK PRIORITIES

Many tasking systems include the concept of a task priority, which indicates the relative importance of this task with respect to others when it comes to processor scheduling. Ada allows the programmer to specify a fixed priority for his tasks, if he so wishes, with the pragma:

pragma PRIORITY (*static_expression*);

placed in the task specification (or in the outermost declarative part, if we are setting the priority for a main program). Note that the priority is fixed at compile-time, with lower values indicating lower priories than higher numbers. The priority number is an integer value of the predefined subtype PRIORITY, whose range is implementation dependent.

The final note on priorities concerns the priority at which a rendezvous is executed. If either or both of the tasks involved in the rendezvous has a defined priority, then it is executed with the higher of the priorities. If neither of the tasks has a defined priority, then the priority at which the rendezvous is executed is similarly undefined.

CHAPTER 10

Structure, Scope and Visibility

In this chapter, we shall draw together the threads of the previous chapters to describe the structure of Ada program units and the interactions between such units and the scope and visibility of identifiers.

10.1 PROGRAM STRUCTURE

In the previous chapters, we have always dealt with "program units", "library units", etc. It is now time to define an Ada program, and see how the units we have encountered go to make up such a program.

In Ada, a program is defined to be a number (one or more) of "complication units", the components of each compilation unit being compiled at the same time. The syntax for a compilation is as follows:

compilation ::= { *compilation_unit* }

compilation_unit ::=
    context_specification subprogram_declaration
  | *context_specification subprogram_body*
  | *context_specification package_declaration*
  | *context_specification package_body*
  | *context_specification subunit*

context_specification ::= { *with_clause* [*use_clause*] }

with_clause ::= **with** *unit_name* { , *unit_name* };

In its simplest form, a program can consist of a single compilation unit, as in the example below:

```
with text_io;
procedure temperature_conversion is
    use text_io;
    package real_io is new float_io(float);
    use real_io;
    Fahrenheit, Celsius : float;
```

```
begin
    get(Fahrenheit);
    Celsius := (Fahrenheit − 32.0) * 5.0 / 9.0;
    put(Celsius);
    put(newline);
end temperature_conversion;
```

Note that there is an implicit declaration of the package STANDARD at the outermost level of every compilation unit, so that the identifiers which are in the visible part of STANDARD are available to all compilations. It is via this mechanism that we can use the identifier for the type "*float*", for example, which is declared in STANDARD.

Unfortunately, real life is never as simple as the example given above, so before we consider a more realistic example, let us define a few terms:

program library   The compilation units which go to make up a program are said to belong to a program library.

library unit   A compilation unit is said to be a library unit if it is not a subunit of another unit.

subunit   The body of a subprogram, package or task which is compiled separately from the compilation unit in which is declared is said to be a subunit of the declaring unit.

Let us now examine a sample compilation to see how a monolithic block of code can be broken up into compilation units and how the compilation units relate to the three definitions above:

```
procedure screen_io is
    package cursor is
        x_coord : integer range 0 . . 79;
        y_coord : integer range 0 . . 23;
        procedure home;
            . . .
    end cursor;
    package body cursor is
        procedure home is
        begin
            x_coord := 0;
            y_coord := 0;
                . . .
        end home;
    begin
        home;
    end cursor;
    procedure move(x, y : integer) is
        use cursor;
```

```
    begin
        x_coord := x ;
        y_coord := y ;
    end move ;
begin
    cursor . home ;
        . . .
end screen_io ;
```

The example above is a complete program, consisting of a single compilation unit. It is also a program library and a library unit, according to the previous definitions. Let us now take the same program and break it up into three separate compilation units, as follows:

```
with cursor ;
procedure screen_io is
    procedure move(x, y : integer) is
        use cursor ;
    begin
        x_coord := x ;
        y_coord := y ;
            . . .
    end move ;
begin
    cursor . home ;
        . . .
end screen ;
```

for the "main program",

```
package cursor is
    x_coord : integer range 0 . . 79 ;
    y_coord : integer range 0 . . 23 ;
    procedure home ;
        . . .
end cursor ;
```

for the package specification and

```
package body cursor is
    procedure home is
    begin
        x_coord := 0 ;
        y_coord := 0 ;
            . . .
    end home ;
```

begin
    home;
end *cursor*;

for the package body. These, then, are compilation units which may now be compiled separately. Together they make up a program library. The "main program" and the package specification are library units and the package body, if it is compiled separately, would be a subunit of the unit which declared it (in this case the unit containing the package specification). Note that in their present form, the package specification and the package body require further modifications in order to compile them separately (see section 10.2).

10.1.1 The With Clause

The elaboration of a **with** clause causes the library units named by it to be implicitly declared immediately after the declaration of the package STANDARD. Thus, the named units are made directly visible, unless they are hidden by some other mechanism. This overcomes a major problem when we split up the original program into individual compilation units, namely the visibility of identifiers in one unit from another. If we take a look at the main program, it can be seen that it was necessary to add a **with** clause to it in order to allow references to the package "*cursor*" in the **use** clause and also to the identifier "*home*" (which is defined in "*cursor*").

Note that any given unit should only specify in a **with** clause those units which are directly required. Thus, "*screen_io*" should only specify "*cursor*" in its **with** clause, and not any units which "*cursor*" requires.

10.2 SUBUNITS

It is possible in Ada to separate the body of a subprogram, package or task from the unit in which it is declared. This makes it a "*subunit*" of the declaring unit, its syntax being:

    subunit ::= **separate** (*unit_name*) *body*

In order to complete the linkage between the subunit and the declaring unit, a "*body stub*" is placed in the declaring unit where the body would normally go. Its syntax is:

    body_stub ::=
        subprogram_specification **is separate**;
     | **package body** *identifier* **is separate**;
     | **task body** *identifier* **is separate**;

To illustrate the point, let us rewrite the original example, making the package body of the package *"cursor"* into a subunit, as follows:

```
procedure screen_io is
    package cursor is
        x_coord : integer range 0 .. 79;
        y_coord : integer range 0 .. 23;
        procedure home;
        . . .
    end cursor;
    package body cursor is separate;
    procedure move(x, y : integer) is
        use cursor;
    begin
        x_coord := x;
        y_coord := y;
        . . .
    end move;
begin
    cursor . home;
    . . .
end screen;
```

for the main program and

```
separate (screen_io);
package body cursor is
    procedure home is
    begin
        x_coord := 0;
        y_coord := 0;
        . . .
    end home;
begin
    home;
end cursor;
```

The important points to note about the example are that the parent unit has to mention the subunit in the body stub and that the subunit has similarly to mention the parent unit to which it belongs. In addition, if the parent unit is itself a subunit, then its full name must be given (as a selected component) in the subunit.

As you would expect, Ada requires that the names of all subunits of a single library unit have to be distinct, to prevent any ambiguities. However, it is perfectly acceptable for subunits of *different* library units in the same program library to have the same name, since the full names will be different. For example, we could have two subunits called *"page_up"*, one a subunit of the library unit *"crt_io"* and the other of *"printer_io"*. Their full names, *"crt_io . page_up"* and *"printer_io . page_up"* are still distinct.

From the point of view of visibility, anything visible from the body stub in the declaring unit is visible to the subunit. Thus, any library units which are made visible to the declaring unit, via a **with** clause, will also be visible to the subunit. In a similar fashion, if any library units are mentioned in the context specification of the subunit, these are directly visible within the subunit.

10.3 IDENTIFIER SCOPE AND VISIBILITY

Having delved into the problems of visibility of identifiers between compilation units, it is now time to focus our attention on the rules governing the visibility of identifiers within these units.

10.3.1 Scope of Identifiers

The purpose of a declaration is to pass information about the declared entity (object, type, subprogram, etc.) to the Ada compiler. A part of this information is the identifier by which other parts of the program text may reference the given entity. For the remainder of this chapter, we shall be examining the concepts of the "scope" and "visibility" of declarations.

The "scope" of a declaration is defined to be the range of program text over which the declaration has an effect. In contrast, a declaration is said to be "visible" from a particular point if the use of the identifier at that point refers to that entity. To illustrate the point, consider the following example:

```
outer:
    declare
        a, b, c : integer;
    begin
        . . .
        a := b;
        . . .
inner:
        declare
            x, y, z : integer;
        begin
            . . .
            x := y;
            z := a;
            . . .
        end inner;
        . . .
        c := z; -- Illegal
        . . .
    end outer;
```

The scope of the declarations of "*a*", "*b*" and "*c*" is from the point of their declaration to the end of the block "*outer*", whilst that of "*x*", "*y*" and "*z*" is from their declaration to the end of the block "*inner*". It can thus be seen that the assignment statement *c*:=*z*; is illegal, since there is no object "*z*" which is in scope.

To give the rules in a more formal manner, the following excerpt from the *Reference Manual for the Ada Programming Language* defines the scoping rules:

(a) The scope of a declaration given in the declarative part of a block or in the declarative part of the body of a subprogram, package or task extends from the declaration to the end of the block, subprogram, package or task.

(b) The scope of a declaration given in the visible part of a package extends from the declaration to the end of the scope of the package declaration itself. It therefore includes the corresponding package body.

(c) The scope of a declaration given in the private part of a package extends from the declaration to the end of the package specification; it also extends over the corresponding package body.

(d) The scope of an entry declaration given in a task specification extends from the declaration to the end of the scope of the task declaration. It therefore includes the corresponding task body.

(e) The scope of a separately compiled subprogram or package, other than a subunit, comprises that compilation unit, its subunits (if any), any other compilation unit that mentions the name of the subprogram or package in a with clause, and the body of this subprogram or package.

(f) The scope of a record component extends from the component declaration to the end of the scope of the record type declaration.

(g) The scope of a discriminant extends from the discriminant declaration to the end of the scope of the corresponding type declaration.

(h) The scope of a formal parameter of a subprogram, entry or generic program unit extends from the parameter declaration to the end of the scope of the declaration of the subprogram, entry or generic program unit itself. It therefore includes the body of the corresponding subprogram or generic program unit, and, for an entry, the corresponding accept statements.

(i) The scope of a loop parameter extends from its occurrence in an iteration clause to the end of the corresponding loop.

(j) The scope of an enumeration literal extends from its occurrence in the corresponding enumeration type declaration to the end of the scope of the enumeration type declaration itself.

To illustrate some of these rules, consider the examples given below:

outer:
    declare
        a, b, c : *integer*;   -- Scope of *a, b, c* starts
    begin
        . . .
        $a := b$;
        . . .

inner:
        declare
            x, y, z : *integer*;   -- Scope of *x, y, z* starts
        begin
            . . .
            $x := y$;
            $z := a$;
            $c := z$;
            . . .
        end *inner*;   -- Scope of *x, y, z* ends
        . . .
        $c := a$;
        . . .
    end *outer*;   -- Scope of *a, b, c* ends
    procedure *x* (*a* : **in out** *integer*) **is**   -- Scope of *a* starts
        temp : *integer*:   -- Scope of *temp* starts
        . . .
    begin
        . . .
        for *i* **in** 1 . . 10 **loop**   -- Scope of *i* starts
        . . .
        end loop;   -- Scope of *i* ends
        . . .
    end *x*;   -- Scope of *a, temp* ends

    package *complex_addition* **is**
        type *complex* **is private**;   -- Scope of *complex* starts
        function "+" (*a, b* : *complex*)
                     return *complex*;
        . . .

```
    private
        type complex is
            record
                    re : float := 0.0;        -- Scope of re starts
                    im : float := 0.0;        -- Scope of im starts
            end record;
    end complex_addition;

    package body complex_addition is
        . . .
    end complex_addition;                     -- Scope of re, im ends

    procedure xyz is
        use complex_addition;                 -- Scope of complex starts
                                              -- Note: re and im are
                                              -- not in scope here.
    begin
        . . .
    end xyz;                                  -- Scope of complex ends
```

The main point which differentiates scope from visibility is that an identifier has the *potential* to be visible from any point which is within its scope, but whether it is actually visible at a particular point depends on a number of other factors, which will be covered in the next section.

10.3.2 Visibility of Identifiers

We now turn our attention to a discussion of the visibility and hiding rules in Ada. Given an identifier which is in scope, they define whether the identifier is visible at a particular point in the program text, or whether it is hidden.

The best way to introduce the concept of hiding is by way of an example:

```
outer:
    declare
        a, b, c : integer;
    begin
        . . .
        a := 1;
        . . .
inner:
        declare
            x, y, z : integer;
            a : integer := -1;
        begin
            . . .
            z := a;
```

> ...
> **end** *inner*;
>
> ...
> **end** *outer*;

It is not obvious from looking at the program text just what will happen as a result of executing the statement $z := a$;. The question at issue is which of the two entities called *"a"* will be used, and thus whether the value of z is +1 or −1 after the assignment.

The resolution of this problem lies in the concept of "hiding" of identifiers. When there is a clash of identifiers, as we have in the example, the hiding rules state that the declaration of an object in an inner block which has the same identifier as an object in an outer block "hides" the outer identifier from direct view. Thus, in the example, after executing $z := a$;, the value of z would be −1.

Again, the visibility rules as stated in the Reference Manual for the Ada Programming Language are:

(a) An identifier declared in the declarative part of a block or in that of of the body of a subprogram, package or task is directly visible within this block or body.

(b) An identifier declared in the visible part of a package is directly visible within the package specification and body.
Outside the package, but within its scope, such an identifier is made visible by a selected component whose prefix names the package. The identifier can also be made directly visible by means of a use clause.

(c) An identifier declared in the private part of a package is directly visible within the package private part and body.

(d) An (entry) identifier declared in a task specification is directly visible within the task specification and body.
Outside the task, but within its scope, the identifier is made visible by a selected component whose prefix names the task or a task object of the task type.

(e) The identifier of a separately compiled subprogram or package is directly visible within the compilation unit itself and its subunits, and within any other compilation unit that has a with clause which mentions the identifier.

(f) The identifier of a record component is directly visible within the record type definition that declares the component, and within a record type representation specification for the record type.

Outside the record type definition, but within the scope of that definition, a record component is made visible by a selected component whose prefix names a record of the type of which it is a component. It is also visible as a choice in a component association of an aggregate of the record type.

(g) The identifier of a discriminant is directly visible within the discriminant part that declares the discriminant and within the associated record type definition.

Where it is not directly visible, but within the scope of the type, a discriminant is made visible by being in a selected component or in an aggregate, as for any other record component. It is also visible at the place of a discriminant name in a named discriminant specification of a discriminant constraint.

(h) The identifier of a formal parameter of a subprogram is directly visible within the formal part where the parameter is declared and within the subprogram body. The identifier of a formal parameter of an entry is directly visible within the formal part where the parameter is declared and within any accept statement for the entry. The identifier of a generic formal parameter is directly visible within the generic part where the parameter is declared and within the specification and body of the generic subprogram or package.

(i) The identifier of a loop parameter is directly visible within the loop where it is declared.

(j) An enumeration literal is directly visible within the scope of the enumeration type that declares the literal.

In certain cases, it is desirable to be able to access a hidden identifier. Notice that the rules specified above only apply to *direct* visibility, i.e. the use of the identifier alone to access the desired object. Hidden identifiers can usually be accessed by applying a qualifier, perhaps a selected component or a discriminant name.

The following are a few examples which illustrate some of the foregoing rules:

```
procedure matrix_invert is
    a, b : matrix;

procedure matrix_multiply is
    b, c : matrix;
begin
    . . .
    b := c;
    . . .
```

$c := matrix\_invert . b$;   – – Use of selected component
                                    – – to access hidden identifier.

          . . .

     end *matrix_multiply*;

begin

     . . .

end *matrix_invert*;

procedure *a* **is**

     package *short_vectors* **is**
          type *short_vec* **is** . . . ;
          . . .
     end *short_vectors*;

     package *long_vectors* **is**
          type *long_vec* **is** . . . ;
          . . .
     end *long_vectors*;

     use *short_vectors*;   – – Makes *short_vec* directly
                                       – – visible.

     x : *short_vec*;   – – We can now use just the
                                       – – identifier.

     y : *long_vectors . long_vec*; – – Here, the identifier is
                                       – – not directly visible, so
                                       – – we must use a selected
                                       – – component.

begin

     . . .

end *a*;

– – First compilation unit:
package misc **is**
     procedure *init*;
     . . .
end *misc*;

package body *misc* **is**
     procedure *init* **is** . . . **end** *init*;
     . . .
end *misc*;

```
- - Second compilation unit :
with misc;                              - - Makes identifiers from misc
                                        - - directly visible.

procedure main_prog is
begin
        init;                           - - We can now use identifier
                                        - - alone.


        . . .
end main_prog;
```

10.3.3 Overloading of Identifiers

In all of the text and examples up to this point, we have taken no account of the possibility of identifiers being overloaded. Overloading of an identifier implies that several entities may be refered to by the same identifier, which seem to contradict the visibility rules.

For subprograms, the declaration of a subprogram is said to hide a previous declaration of a subprogram with the same identifier *only* if the order, names and types of the parameters (and for functions, the types of the results) are the same, and the same parameters have default values (see Chapter 5, section 5.6). If these criteria are not met, then the second declaration overloads but does not hide the first. In a similar fashion, enumeration literals may be over-loaded where their scope overlap. Ambiguities are then resolved by the use of a qualified expression.

If overloading occurs in an expression as the result of a **use** clause, then the identifiers which are introduced by the **use** clause are only considered during conflict resolution if there is no other way to uniquely determine the referenced entity.

10.4 RENAMING DECLARATIONS

The renaming declaration is used to introduce an additional name for an entity. The old name is still available and in no way influenced by the new one. The syntax for a renaming declaration is:

```
renaming_declaration ::=
        identifier : type_mark renames name;
    |   identifier : exception renames name;
    |   package identifier renames name;
    |   task identifier renames name;
    |   subprogram_specification renames name;
```

In all of the different types of renaming declaration given above, there must be compatibility between the renaming declaration and the original declaration.

It would be illegal, for example, to have the following:

declare
> *a_very_long_name_to_type* : *integer*;
> *avlntt* : *float* **renames** *a_very_long_name_to_type*;
> -- Illegal, the types don't agree

begin
> . . .

end;

Note that there is the obvious constraint that a renaming declaration which renames a subprogram must be able to uniquely determine a single subprogram from the name and specification. If there is more than one visible subprogram with specifications and identifiers which match the renaming declaration then the renamining declaration is illegal.

CHAPTER 11

Input-Output

In this final chapter, we shall cover the Ada input-output facilities, which are a defined part of the languages, unlike Algol-60, for example.

11.1 OVERVIEW

Ada provides two packages to assist in performing input-output functions, the package INPUT_OUTPUT to support high-level I/O to files and the package TEXT_IO to support the more primative operations.

11.2 FILES AND FILE NAMES

There are two kinds of files in Ada, internal files and external files. An internal file is a declared object which has a name and a file-type associated with it. The file type, IN_FILE, INOUT_FILE or OUT_FILE is used to specify the kinds of transfers which are allowed for the named file (in much the same manner as the modes for subprogram parameters), providing the classical READ, READ/WRITE and WRITE access mechanisms. An external file is where the information actually resides, and is specified by implementation dependent information such as device name, unit number, etc. This information is contained in the name of the external file, which takes the form of an implementation dependent text string. The linkage between an internal file and an external file is established by calls to the CREATE or OPEN procedures.

A file consists of a sequence of elements, all elements being of the same type. There are many different types, and hence file I/O is supported by a generic package called INPUT_OUTPUT, with an instantiation of the package being required for each element type to be used. Once the instantiation has taken place, the user can then declare internal files for that element type and use the subprograms provided by the instantiation to manipulate the files. To illustrate:

declare

    package *integer_io* **is new** INPUT_OUTPUT(*integer*);
    package   *float_io* **is new** INPUT_OUTPUT(*float*);

    from_ file : *integer_io* . *in_ file* ; - - Note file-type
      to_ file :   *float_io* . *out_ file*;

    i : *integer*;
    f : *float*;

begin

    . . .
    integer_io . OPEN (*file* => *from_ file*,
                 name => "SY :OLD . DAT; 1");

    float_io . CREAT (*file* => *to_ file*,
                 name => "SY:NEW . DAT; 1"):

    . . .
    integer_io . READ (*from_ file*, *i*);
    f := *float*(*i*);
    float_io . WRITE (*to_ file*, *f*);
    . . .
      float_io . CLOSE (*to_ file*);
    integer_io . CLOSE (*from_ file*);
end;

11.2.1 Opening, Closing and Testing Files

In the example given above, it was necessary to establish a link between the internal file name and the external file before we could access it. This is effected by calling either the OPEN or CREATE procedures, depending on whether or not the external file already exists. The procedure specifications for these two procedures are:

    procedure CREATE (*file* : **in out**   *out_ file* ;
                    name : **in**   *string*) ;

    procedure CREATE (*file* : **in out** *inout_ file* ;
                    name : **in**   *string*) ;

    procedure OPEN (*file* : **in out**   *in_ file* ;
                 name : **in**   *string*) ;

    procedure OPEN (*file* : **in out**   *out_ file* ;
                 name : **in**   *string*) ;

    procedure OPEN (*file* : **in out** *inout_ file* ;
                 name : **in**   *string*) ;

A call to the CREATE procedure will cause a new external file to be created and a linkage to be made between the new external file and the named internal file. Upon a successful return from the call, the external file is linked to the internal file, which is said to be "open" when such a linkage exists. If for any reason the external file cannot be created the exception NAME_ERROR is raised. If the internal file is already open, then the exception STATUS_ERROR is raised. Note that the file-type of the internal file used in a call to CREATE must obviously be either OUT_FILE or INOUT_FILE, because it does not sense to try to read from a file which contains no data.

A call to OPEN makes the linkage to an existing external file (rather that creating a new one), thus "opening" the internal file. If the external file does not exist, then the exception NAME_ERROR is raised, while if the internal file is already open the exception STATUS_ERROR is raised. In this case, there is no restriction on the file-type of the internal file.

It would be useful if the programmer could find out whether a given internal file was already open before trying to open it with CREATE or OPEN. The function IS_OPEN does this. Its specifications are:

function IS_OPEN (*file* : **in**   *in_file*) **return** *boolean*;
function IS_OPEN (*file* : **in**   *out_file*) **return** *boolean*;
function IS_OPEN (*file* : **in** *inout_file*) **return** *boolean*;

A call to this function, with an internal file name as a parameter, will return the boolean value TRUE if the internal file is open (associated with an external file) and FALSE otherwise. We could thus write:

```
declare
    package x_io is new input_output(x);
    use x_io ;
    my_file : x_io . in_file;
    . . .
begin
    . . .
    if is_open(my_file) then
        . . .
    else
        open(my_file, "MT:");
    end if;
    . . .
end;
```

When the programmer has finished processing a file, the linkage between the internal and external files can be broken. This is done by calling the procedure

CLOSE with an internal file name as a parameter. The specifications for CLOSE are:

>   **procedure** CLOSE (*file* : **in out**   *in_ file*);
>   **procedure** CLOSE (*file* : **in out**   *out_ file*);
>   **procedure** CLOSE (*file* : **in out** *inout_ file*);

If the internal file is already closed the exception STATUS_ERROR is raised.

There are two further subprograms which deal with external files in the package INPUT_OUTPUT, NAME and DELETE. The purpose of the function NAME is to return a string representing the external file which is linked to the internal file given as a parameter. The specifications for NAME are:

>   **function** NAME (*file* : **in**   *in_ file*) **return** *string*;
>   **function** NAME (*file* : **in**   *out_ file*) **return** *string*;
>   **function** NAME (*file* : **in** *inout_ file*) **return** *string*;

Note that the string which is returned is obviously implementation dependent and that the STATUS_ERROR exception is raised by the function if the internal file passed as a parameter is closed.

The DELETE procedure is used to delete an external file. Its specification is:

>   **procedure** DELETE (*name* : **in** *string*);

A call to DELETE does not guarantee that the named file is immediately deleted, only that no further OPENs can be performed on that file. It is easy to think of situations wherein a single external file may be linked to several internal files. Under these circumstances all linkages must be broken before the file can actually be deleted. The NAME_ERROR exception is raised if the file cannot be deleted for any reason (e.g. it does not exist, is protected, etc.).

11.3 INPUT-OUTPUT WITH FILES

The previous section introduced the mechanisms by which we could name files and make the necessary linkages between the language and the actual storage media. In this section we shall explore the facilities for reading from and writing to files, as well as positioning within files. Note that the procedure and function specifications in this section are given only for the file-type parameters IN_FILE and OUT_FILE, since for every subprogram which can take an IN_FILE parameter there is a subprogram which can take an INOUT_FILE parameter, and similarly with OUT_FILE.

As previous stated, a file is considered to be a series of elements, each having an associated sequence number belonging to the implementation dependent type FILE_INDEX (all positions within files are specified as integers belonging to this type). Note that not all elements are necessarily defined. In an indexed file, for example, there may be sequence numbers for which there are no keys.

For each open internal file there is an associated "current position" for either reading or writing (depending on the file-type), which refers to the element which will be referenced by the next read or write operation. When a file is first opened, the current position is set to the "beginning" of the file. For reading, this means that the current position is set to 1 (or, if there is no defined element corresponding to that sequence number, the first defined one), and for writing the current position is set to 1.

There are two further properties of a file, in addition to the current position. These are the "current size" and "end position". The current size is the number of defined elements in the file and the end position is the sequence number of the last defined element. If a file has no defined elements, both of these are zero.

There are two procedures provided to effect transfers of information to or from a file, READ and WRITE.

procedure READ (*file* :   **in**   *in- file*   ;
                        item : **out** *element_type*);

procedure WRITE (*file* : **in**   *out_ file*   ;
                        item : **in** *element_type*);

The READ procedure returns the value of the element at the current read position in the *"item"* parameter, setting the current read position to the position of the next defined element. If there is no such element, then the position is incremented by 1. If an attempt is made to read an undefined element, then the DATA_ERROR exception will be raised. Similarly, an attempt to read from beyond the end of the file (current read position greater than end position) will raise the END_ERROR exception.

The complementary WRITE procedure takes the value of the *"item"* parameter, writes it to the file at the current write position and then increments the current write position. If this write overwrites an undefined element, thus increasing the number of defined elements in the file, then the current file size is also incremented. If current write position *before* the write was greater than the end position, then the end position is updated with the value of the old current write position.

To draw together the threads of the previous paragraphs, let us use the example of reading file of integers, squaring them and writing the results to a new file:

declare
        package *my_io* **is new** *input_output(integer)*;
        use *my_io* ;
        destination : *out_file*;
            source : *in_file*;
            temp   : *integer*;

```
begin
    open(source, "/usr/source/integers");
    create(destination, "/usr/dest/integers");

    read(source, temp);
    temp := temp * temp;
    write(destination, temp);

    close(source);
    close(destination);
end;
```

The example, as it is written, is only useful for squaring the first element of the source file. To make it really useful, we need to be able to loop through all of the defined elements. There are several functions which might help us in this regard. The first of these is the function which tests for the end-of-file:

function END_OF_FILE (*file* : **in** *in_file*) **return** *boolean*;

This function returns the boolean value "*true*" if the current read position of the given file is greater than its end position. We can now rewrite the example as follows:

```
declare
    package my_io is new input_output(integer);
    use my_io;
    destination : out_file;
        source : in_file;
         temp : integer;
begin
    open(source, "/usr/source/integers");
    create(destination, "/usr/dest/integers");
    while not end_of_file(source) loop
        read(source, temp);
        temp := temp * temp;
        write(destination, temp);
    end loop;
    close(source);
    close(destination);
end;
```

The other functions which allow the programmer to inquire about the current state of a file are:

function SIZE (*file* : **in**   *in_file*) **return** *file_index*;
function SIZE (*file* : **in** *out_file*) **return** *file_index*;

which would enable us to determine the number of defined elements in the file,

> **function** LAST (*file* : **in**   *in_file*) **return** *file_index* ;
> **function** LAST (*file* : **in** *out_file*) **return** *file_index* ;

which returns the sequence number of the end position, and lastly the functions NEXT_READ and NEXT_WRITE:

> **function** NEXT_READ (*file* : **in**   *in_file*) **return** *file_index* ;
> **function** NEXT_WRITE (*file* : **in** *out_file*) **return** *file_index* ;

which return the sequence number of the current read or write position.

Ada provides the capability to manipulate a file by changing the values of the current position and the size and end position of a file. The procedures which perform these actions are:

> **procedure** SET_READ (*file* : **in**   *in_file*   ;
>   *to* : **in** *file_index*);
> **procedure** SET_WRITE (*file* : **in**   *out_file* ;
>   *to* : **in** *file_index*);

which set the current read position or current write position to the value specified by the "*to*" parameter. The special case of setting these to the start of a file (analogous to the Fortran REWIND) can be handled by the procedures:

> **procedure** RESET_READ (*file* **in** *in_file*);

which sets the current read position to the first defined element, or to 1 if none are defined, and

> **procedure** RESET_WRITE (*file* : **in** *out_file*);

which sets the current write position to 1. The final file manipulation procedure is:

> **procedure** TRUNCATE (*file* : **in**   *out_file* ;
>   *to* : **in** *file_index*);

which sets the end position of the file to the specified value. If necessary, the file size is also modified. Note that this procedure cannot be used to extend a file, since the exception USE_ERROR is raised if the value of the "*to*" parameter is greater than the current end position.

A final word of caution before we turn to text-I/O. The programmer should be aware of the possibility that an I/O operation will be attempted which cannot be completed, perhaps because a physical device does not support that operation. Examples might be an attempt to write to keyboard or to access a device which is offline. Under such circumstances, the DEVICE_ERROR exception will be raised.

11.4 THE PACKAGE TEXT IO

The previous section dealt with I/O to files, with there being no mention of the external representation of the data. The package TEXT_IO, however, supports I/O in a readable form, performing any necessary conversions between the internal and external representations. The differences between the functions provided by the package INPUT_OUTPUT and those provided by TEXT_IO are similar to the differences between the Fortran "unformatted" and "formatted" I/O.

The TEXT_IO packages consists of 4 generic packages and some subprograms. There is a generic package for integers, INTEGER_IO, a generic package for floating-point I/O, FLOAT_IO a generic package for fixed-point I/O, FIXED_IO and a generic package for I/O of enumeration types, ENUMERATION_IO. In addition, there are several subprograms which deal with character handling, string handling, I/O of booleans, layout functions and file manipulation. The bulk of the work in the package is performed by the overloaded subprograms GET and PUT.

11.4.1 Standard Input and Standard Output

Unlike the file I/O package, INPUT_OUTPUT, which requires that every subprogram be passed in internal file as a parameter, the TEXT_IO package uses the concept of a default source file for input and a default destination file for output. These are linked to two implementation dependent files at the start of a program, and are thus initially open. This allows there to be a short form of the GET and PUT procedures which needs no explicit file, while still allowing the use of the long form. Therefore, for a given type "*x*", the GET procedure would have two forms:

```
procedure GET (item : out x);
procedure GET (file : in in_file  ;
               item : out    x ) ;
```

There would similarly be two forms for the PUT procedure, a long one with a file parameter and a short one without. For the remainder of this chapter, only the short form of each subprogram specification will be given, the long form being assumed to take a file parameter of the appropriate file-type (IN_FILE for GET and OUT_FILE for PUT, etc.).

An additional difference between the two packages is that INPUT_OUTPUT will work with all file types, whereas TEXT_IO only works for the IN_FILE and OUT_FILE file-types. The result of using a TEXT_IO subprogram with an INOUT_FILE file-type is undefined.

To support the default file facilities, TEXT_IO provides the following subprograms for manipulation of default file settings:

```
function   STANDARD_INPUT return  in_file;
function STANDARD_OUTPUT return out_file;
```

which return the initial assignments for the default input and output files, respectively, the two functions:

> **function**   CURRENT_INPUT **return**   *in_file*;
> **function** CURRENT_OUTPUT **return** *out_file*;

which return the current settings of the default input and default output files and the procedures:

> **procedure**   SET_INPUT (*file* : **in**   *in_file*);
> **procedure** SET_OUTPUT (*file* : **in** *out_file*);

which can be used to change the settings for default input and output files.

11.4.2 Text File Layout

Before we enter into a discussion of the I/O facilities for the various types, it is necessary to understand the Ada rules regarding the layout of text files.

In the same way that READ and WRITE, in the sections on file I/O, have a current position upon which they act, GET and PUT also have a current position on which they act. For text files, the current position is specified in terms of a "current line number" and a "current column number", both of which range from 1 upwards. There is no restriction as to line length (other than that it must be less than or equal to the file size), nor need the line length be fixed throughout a file. The programmer is free to mix short and long lines within a file. Support for layout control is achieved via the following subprograms:

> **function**   COL **return** *natural*;
> **procedure** SET_COL (*to* : **in** *natural*);

which get and set the current column number,

> **function** LINE **return** *natural*;

which returns the current line number,

> **function**   LINE_LENGTH **return** *integer*;
> **procedure** SET_LINE_LENGTH (*n* : **in** *integer*);

which return and set the current line length (a line length of zero indicates that the line length is unset, the initial condition when a file is opened),

> **procedure** NEW_LINE (*spacing* : **in** *natural* := 1);

which terminates the current line (padding with blanks to the current line length, if necessary), resets the current column number to 1 and adds "*spacing*" lines (note the default value of 1). This procedure is only valid for the default output file, or a file whose file type is OUT_FILE. There is a complementary procedure for the default input file (or IN_FILE files):

> **procedure** SKIP_FILE (*spacing* : **in** *natural* := 1);

and finally for the default input file (or IN_FILE files), there is:

function END_OF_LINE **return** *boolean*;

which returns the boolean value *"true"* if the are no remaining characters to be read from the current line. Some examples which illustrate the use of the these subprograms are:

```
procedure main is
    use text_io;
    old_input, new_input : in_file;
    . . .
begin
    . . .
    old_input := standard_input( );
    set_input (new_input);
    . . .
end main;

procedure test_page (n : in natural) is
    use text_io;
    page_size : constant natural := 52;
begin
    if ( line( )+n ) > page_size
    then
        - - Page up, print headers and reset counters
    end if;
end test_page;
```

11.4.3 Integer I/O

Input and output for an integer type is supported by an instance of the generic package INTEGER_IO created for the given type. If we wished to work with the type *"natural"*, the instantiation:

package *nat_io* **is new** *integer_io(natural)*;

provides us with the procedures GET and PUT for the type *"natural"*. The subprogram specifications for the short forms of the two procedures are:

procedure GET (*item* : **out** *i_type*);

procedure PUT (*item* : **in** *i_type*;
                        width : **in** *integer* := 0;
                        base : **in** *integer* **range** 2 .. 16 := 10);

The GET procedure will ignore leading layout characters such as tabs, spaces and line-marks, after which it will read from the input file (either default input for the short form or the *in_file* parameter for the long form), performing a conversion from the text to the required type and placing the resulting value in the *"item"* parameter. As you would expect, a single sign character, + or −, may precede the digits and the exception CONSTRAINT_ERROR will be raised if the item parameter cannot hold the final value.

The PUT procedure performs the reverse function, converting the internal value of the *"item"* parameter into a sequence of characters and writing them to the output file.

The optional *"width"* parameter can be used to specify the minimum number of characters the programmer wishes the subprogram to generate. If the width parameter is too small to allow representation of the value in *"item"*, then it will be ignored. If it is larger than required, leading spaces will be added.

The *"base"* parameter is also optional, its default being 10. If it is used, then the number is output according to the syntax for a based number (see Appendix A), in the form:

> *base # number # exponent*

Some examples of the output conversions are:

```
put(5);                          -- "5"
put( item => 5,
     width => 3 );               -- "5"
put( item => 5,
     width => 7,
     base => 2  );               -- "2#101#"
put(−5);                         -- "−5", (this example is invalid for
                                    values of the type "natural")
```

11.4.4 Floating-Point I/O
Floating point I/O is supported by instances of the generic package FLOAT_IO. The procedures work in a very similar way to those used for the integers. Their specifications are:

> **procedure** GET (*item* : **out** *fl_type*);

> **procedure** PUT   (*item*   : **in** *fl_type*;
> width   : **in** *integer* := 0;
> mantissa   : **in** *integer* := *fl_type'digits*;
> exponent   : **in** *integer* := 2);

The item and width parameters perform the same functions as before. The floating point numbers are output in the form "−1.23456E−78", with control

over the number of digits in the mantissa (excluding any leading "–" and the ".")
being exercised by the value of the optional *"mantissa"* parameter. There is
similar control over the number of digits in the exponent (excluding the "E"
and any "–") provided by the *"exponent"* parameter. Some examples of floating
point I/O are:

```
declare
     type fl_type is digits 8;
     package fl_io is new float_io(f 1_type);
     use fl_io;
     pi : fl_type := 3.141593;
begin
     put(pi);                          -- "3.1415930E00"
     pi := pi / 10.0;
     put(item => pi,
         mantissa => 4,               -- Note omission of a parameter.
         exponent => 2 );             -- "3.142E-01", note rounding.
     put(item => pi,
         width => 10,
         mantissa => 4 );             -- "3.142E-01"
     . . .
end;
```

There are a couple of points about the example which are worth exploring.
Firstly, note that if the *"mantissa"* parameter specifies fewer digits than that
used to represent the type, then rounding will be performed. Secondly, if the
"exponent" parameter is used, and it provides an insufficient number of digits,
then the required number will be used, overriding the given value.

11.4.5 Fixed-Point I/O

The last of the numeric I/O package is the one which supports I/O for fixed-point
types, the generic package FIXED_IO. An instantiation will again provide the
subprograms:

procedure GET (*item* : **out** *fi_type*);

procedure PUT (*item* : **in** *fi_type*;
                    width : **in** *integer* := 0;
                    fract : **in** *integer* := *default_decimals*);

with the *"fract"* parameter specifying the number of digits after the decimal point. For both input and output rounding is performed if necessary. Some examples of fixed-point I/O are:

```
declare
      type fi_type is delta 0.001;
      package fi_io is new fixed_io(fi_type);
      use fi_io;
      score : fi_type := 1.248;
begin
      put(score);                    -- "1.248"
      put(item => score,
          width =>    6 );           -- "1.248"
      put(item => score,
          width =>    6,
          fract =>    2 );           -- "1.25"
      put(item => score,
          width =>    8,
          fract =>    5 );           -- "1.24800"
end;
```

11.4.6 Enumeration I/O

Instantiation of the generic package ENUMERATION_IO provides the usual pair of subprograms to facilitate I/O for the given type. The subprogram specifications for their short forms are:

```
procedure GET (item : out e_type);

procedure PUT (item : in e_type;
               width : in integer := 0;
               lower_case : in boolean := false );
```

For input, GET makes no distinction between upper-case and lower-case characters. The exception DATA_ERROR is raised if there is no match with one of the enumeration literals. On output, PUT uses the parameter "*lower_case*" to specify which case to write the enumeration literal. If the "*width*" parameter is used, and it provides more character positions than are needed, then trailing spaces are appended. Some examples of enumeration I/O are:

```
declare
      type valve_position is ( closed, travelling, open );
      package valve_io is new enumeration_io(valve_position);
      use valve_io;
      var : valve_position := open;
```

```
   begin
        put(var);                              -- "OPEN"
        put(item => var,
            lower_case => true );              -- "open"
        put(item => var,
            width => 5 );                      -- "OPEN  "
   end;
```

11.4.7 Boolean I/O

Booleans are really a special case of enumeration types, so it should come as no surprise that the subprogram specifications differ from those for enumeration types only in type of the *"item"* parameter:

```
procedure GET (item : out boolean);

procedure PUT (item : in boolean;
               width : in integer := 0;
               lower_case : in boolean := false );
```

Note, however, that there is no generic instantiation to be performed. Other than that, I/O for booleans can be treated as I/O for an enumeration type, with the literals being TRUE and FALSE.

11.4.8 Character I/O

Character I/O makes use of the current line number and current column number column number concepts, introduced in section 11.4.2, above. The subprogram specifications for the short forms of the procedures are:

```
procedure GET (item : out character);

procedure PUT (item :   in character);
```

A call to GET will return the value of the character at the current position, incrementing that position afterwards (if the line length of the file is fixed, this may include setting the current position to the start of the next line).

A call to the PUT procedure will write the character in the *"item"* parameter at the current position, incrementing the current position afterwards. If the file has fixed length lines, the increment process may include the appending of a line mark to the end of the current line and setting the current position to the start of a new one.

Note as with GET and PUT for booleans, these procedures are *not* part of a generic package.

11.4.9 String I/O

In addition to providing the primative functions for chatacter I/O, Ada also provides for string and line I/O. The two procedures (four, counting the long forms):

procedure GET (*item* : **out** *string*);

procedure PUT (*item* :   **in** *string*);

read or write to or from the "*item*" parameter. For GET, leading layout characters are ignored and the string is read, up to but not including the next space character. An additional form of GET is provided as a function:

function GET_STRING **return** *string*;

This then allows, for example, the direct concatenation of input strings without having to use intermediate variables. A special case of GET_STRING is also provided:

function GET_LINE **return** *string*;

This function passes back the string representing all characters from the current position up to, but not including the next line-mark. After the call, the current position is at the start of the next line.

The complementary operation is to write a whole line, and this is provided by the subprogram:

procedure PUT_LINE (*item* : **in** *string*);

which takes the string in the "*item*" parameter and writes it to the output file, adding a line mark at the end.

Ada Syntax Definition

---

abort_statement ::= **abort** *task_name* { , *task_name* };

accept_statement ::=
    accept *entry_name* [*formal_part*] [**do**
        sequence_of_statements
    end [*identifier*]];

access_type_definition ::= **access** *subtype_indication*

accuracy_constraint ::=
    floating_point_constraint | *fixed_point_constraint*

actual_parameter ::= *expression*

actual_parameter_part ::=
    (*parameter_association* { , *parameter_association* })

adding_operator ::= + | − | &

address_specification ::= **for** *name* **use at** *static_simple_expression*;

aggregate ::= (*component_association* { , *component_association* })

alignment_clause ::= **at mod** *static_simple_expression*

allocator ::=
    new *type_mark* [(*expression*)]
  | **new** *type_mark* *aggregate*
  | **new** *type_mark* *discriminant_constraint*
  | **new** *type_mark* *index_constraint*

argument ::= [*identifier* =>] *name*
    | [*identifier* =>] *static_expression*

array_type_definition ::=
    array (*index* {, *index* }) **of** *component_subtype_indication*
  | **array** *index_constraint* **of** *component_subtype_indication*

assignment_statement ::= *variable_name* := *expression*;

attribute ::= *name'identifier*

base ::= *integer*

based_integer ::= *extended_digit* { [*underscore*] *extended_digit* }

based_number ::=
    base # *based_integer* [. *based_integer*] # [*exponent*]

basic_loop ::=
    loop
        sequence_of_statements
    end loop

block ::=
    [*block_identifier*:]
    [**declare**
        declarative_part]
    begin
        sequence_of_statements
    [**exception**
        { *exception_handler* }]
    end [*block_identifier*] ;

body ::= *subprogram_body* | *package_body* | *task_body*

body_stub ::=
    subprogram_specification **is separate**;
  | **package body** *identifier* **is separate**;
  | **task body** *identifier* **is separate**;

case_statement ::=
    case *expression* **is**
        { **when** *choice* { | *choice* }=> *sequence_of_statements* }
    end case;

character_string ::= "{*character*}"

choice ::= *simple_expression* | *discrete_range* | **others**

code_statement ::= *qualified_expression*;

compilation ::= {*compilation_unit*}

compilation_unit ::=
    context_specification subprogram_declaration
   | *context_specification subprogram_body*
   | *context_specification package_declaration*
   | *context_specification package_body*
   | *context_specification subunit*

component_association ::=
    [*choice* {| *choice*}=>] *expression*

component_declaration ::=
    identifier_list : *subtype_indication* [:= *expression*] ;
   | *identifier_list* : *array_type_definition* [:= *expression*] ;

component_list ::=
    {*component_declaration*} [*variant_part*] | **null**;

compound_statement ::=
    if_statement | *case_statement*
   | *loop_statement* | *block*
   | *accept_statement* | *select_statement*

condition ::= *boolean_expression*

conditional_entry_call ::=
    select
        entry_call [*sequence_of_statements*]
    else
        sequence_of_statements
    end select;

constraint ::=
    range_constraint | *accuracy_constraint*
   | *index_constraint* | *discriminant_constraint*

context_specification ::= {*with_clause* [*use_clause*] }

decimal_number ::= *integer* [*. integer*] [*exponent*]

declaration ::=
    object_declaration | *number_declaration*
   | *type_declaration* | *subtype_declaration*
   | *subprogram_declaration* | *package_declaration*
   | *task_declaration* | *exception_declaration*
   | *renaming_declaration*

declarative_item ::= *declaration* | *use_clause*

declarative_part ::=
    { *declarative_item* } { *representation_specification* } { *program_component* }

delay_statement ::= **delay** *simple_expression*;

derived_type_definition ::= **new** *subtype_indication*

designator ::= *identifier* | *operator_symbol*

discrete_range ::= *type_mark* [*range_constraint*] | *range*

discriminant_constraint ::=
    (*discriminant_specification* { , *discriminant_specification* })

discriminant_declaration ::=
    identifier_list : *subtype_indication* [:= *expression*]

discriminant_part ::=
    (*discriminant_declaration* { ; *discriminant_declaration* })

discriminant_specification ::=
    [*discriminant_name* { | *discriminant_name* } =>] *expression*

entry_call ::= *entry_name* [*actual_parameter_part*] ;

entry_declaration ::=
    entry *identifier* [(*discrete_range*)] [*formal_part*] ;

enumeration_literal ::= *identifier* | *character_literal*

enumeration_type_definition ::=
    (*enumeration_literal* { , *enumeration_literal* })

enumeration_type_representation ::= **for** *type_name* **use** *aggregate*;

exception_choice ::= *exception_name* | **others**

exception_declaration ::= *identifier_list* : **exception**;

exception_handler ::=
    when *exception_choice* { | *exception_choice* } =>
        sequence_of_statements

exit_statement ::=
    exit [*loop_name*] [**when** *condition*] ;

exponent ::= *E* [+] *integer* | *E* − *integer*

exponentiating_operator ::= ******

expression ::=
    relation { **and** *relation* }
    | *relation* { **or** *relation* }
    | *relation* { **xor** *relation* }
    | *relation* { **and then** *relation* }
    | *relation* { **or else** *relation* }

extended_digit ::= *digit* | *letter*

factor ::= *primary* [****** *primary*]

fixed_point_constraint ::=
    delta *static_simple_expression* [*range_constraint*]

floating_point_constraint ::=
    digits *static_simple_expression* [*range_constraint*]

formal_parameter ::= *identifier*

formal_part ::=
    (*parameter_declaration* { ; *parameter_declaration* })

function_call ::=
    function_name *actual_parameter_part* | *function_name* ( )

generic_actual_parameter ::=
    expression | *subprogram_name* | *subtype_indication*

generic_association ::=
    [*formal_parameter* =>] *generic_actual_parameter*

generic_formal_parameter ::=
    parameter_declaration;
  | **type** *identifier* [*discriminant_part*] **is** *generic_type_definition*;
  | **with** *subprogram_specification* [**is** *name*] ;
  | **with** *subprogram_specification* **is** <>;

generic_instantiation ::=
    new *name* [(*generic_association* { , *generic_association* })]

generic_package_declaration ::=
    generic_part package_specification;

generic_package_instantiation ::=
    package *identifier* **is** *generic_instantiation*;

generic_part ::= **generic** { *generic_formal_parameter* }

generic_subprogram_declaration ::=
    generic_part subprogram_specification;

generic_subprogram_instantiation ::=
    procedure *identifier* **is** *generic_instantiation*;
  | **function** *designator* **is** *generic_instantiation*;

generic_type_definition ::=
    (<>) | **range** <> | **delta** <> | **digits** <>
  | *array_type_definition* | *access_type_definition*
  | *private_type_definition*

goto_statement ::= **goto** *label_name*;

identifier ::= *letter* { [*underscore*] *letter_or_digit* }

identifier_list ::= *identifier* { , *identifier* }

if_statement ::=
    if *condition* **then**
        sequence_of_statements
    { **elsif** *condition* **then**
        sequence_of_statements }
    [**else**
        sequence_of_statements]
    end if;

incomplete_type_declaration ::= **type** *identifier* [*discriminant_part*] ;

index ::= *type_mark* **range** < >

index_constraint ::= (*discrete_range* { , *discrete_range* })

indexed_component ::= *name* (*expression* { , *expression* })

integer ::= *digit* {[*underscore*] *digit* }

integer_type_definition ::= *range_constraint*

iteration_clause ::=
    for *loop_parameter* **in** [**reverse**] *discrete_range*
  | **while** *condition*

label ::= <<*identifier*>>

length_specification ::= **for** *attribute* **use** *expression*;

letter ::= *upper_case_letter* | *lower_case_letter*

letter_or_digit ::= *letter* | *digit*

literal ::=
    numeric_literal | *enumeration_literal* | *character_string* | **null**

location ::= **at** *static_simple_expression* **range** *range*

logical_operator ::= **and** | **or** | **xor**

loop_parameter ::= *identifier*

loop_statement ::=
    [*loop_identifier* :] [*iteration_clause*] *basic_loop* [*loop_identifier*] ;

mode ::= [in] | out | in out

multiplying_operator ::= * | / | mod | rem

name ::= *identifier*
   | *indexed_component* | *slice*
   | *selected_component* | *attribute*
   | *function_call* | *operator_symbol*

null_statement ::= null;

number_declaration ::=
    identifier_list : constant := *literal_expression*;

numeric_literal ::= *decimal_number* | *based_number*

object_declaration ::=
    identifier_list : [constant] *subtype_indication* [:= *expression*];
  | *identifier_list* : [constant] *array_type_definition* [:= *expression*];

operator_symbol ::= *character_string*

package_body ::=
      package body *identifier* is
        declarative_part
      [begin
        sequence_of_statements
      [exception
        { *exception_handler* }]]
      end [*identifier*];

package_declaration ::= *package_specification*;
  | *generic_package_declaration*
  | *generic_package_instantiation*

package_specification ::=
    package *identifier* is
      { *declarative_item* }
    [private
      { *declarative_item* }
      { *representation_specification* }]
    end [*identifier*]

parameter_association ::= [*formal_parameter* =>] *actual_parameter*

parameter_declaration ::=
    identifier_list : *mode subtype_indication* [:= *expression*]

pragma ::= **pragma** *identifier* [(*argument* { , *arguement* })] ;

primary ::=
    literal | *aggregate* | *name* | *allocator* | *function_call*
    | *type_conversion* | *qualified_expression* | (*expression*)

private_type_definition ::= [**limited**] **private**

procedure_call ::= *procedure_name* [*actual_parameter_part*] ;

program_component ::= *body*
    | *package_declaration* | *task_declaration* | *body_stub*

qualified_expression ::=
    type_mark'(*expression*) | *type_mark'aggregate*

raise_statement ::= **raise** [*exception_name*] ;

range ::= *simple_expression* . . *simple_expression*

range_constraint ::= **range** *range*

real_type_definition ::= *accuracy_constraint*

record_type_definition ::=
    record
        component_list
    end record

record_type_representation ::=
    for *type_name* **use**
        record [*alignment_clause*;]
            { *component_name location*; }
        end record;

relation ::=
    simple_expression [*relational_operator simple_expression*]
    | *simple_expression* [**not**] **in** *range*
    | *simple_expression* [**not**] **in** *subtype_indication*

relational_operator ::= = | /= | < | <= | > | >=

renaming_declaration ::=
     identifier : type_mark **renames** *name*;
   | *identifier* : **exception renames** *name*;
   | **package** *identifier* **renames** *name*;
   | **task** *identifier* **renames** *name*;
   | *subprogram_specification* **renames** *name*;

representation_specification ::=
     length_specification | *enumeration_type_representation*
   | *record_type_representation* | *address_specification*

return_statement ::= **return** [*expression*] ;

select_alternative ::=
     accept_statement [*sequence_of_statements*]
   | *delay_statement* [*sequence_of_statements*]
   | **terminate**;

select_statement ::= *selective_wait*
   | *conditional_entry_call* | *timed_entry_call*

selected_component ::=
     name . *identifier* | *name* . **all** | *name* . *operator_symbol*

selective_wait ::=
     select
        [**when** *condition* =>]
           select_alternative
     { **or** [**when** *condition* =>]
           select_alternative }
     [**else**
        sequence_of_statements]
     end select;

sequence_of_statements ::= *statement* { *statement* }

simple_expression ::= [*unary_operator*] *term* { *adding_operator term* }

simple_statement ::= *null_statement*
   | *assignment_statement* | *exit_statement*
   | *return_statement* | *goto_statement*
   | *procedure_call* | *entry_call*
   | *delay_statement* | *abort_statement*
   | *raise_statement* | *code_statement*

slice ::= *name (discrete_range)*

statement ::=
    { *label* } *simple_statement* | { *label* } *compound_statement*

subprogram_body ::=
    subprogram_specification **is**
        declarative_part
    begin
        sequence_of_statements
    [**exception**
        { *exception_handler* }]
    end [*designator*] ;

subprogram_declaration ::= *subprogram_specification* ;
   | *generic_subprogram_declaration*
   | *generic_subprogram_instantiation*

subprogram_specification ::=
    procedure *identifier* [*formal_part*]
   | **function** *designator* [*formal_part*] **return** *subtype_indication*

subtype_declaration ::=
    subtype *identifier* **is** *subtype_indication* ;

subtype_indication ::= *type_mark* [*constraint*]

subunit ::= **separate** (*unit_name*) *body*

task_body ::=
    task body *identifier* **is**
        [*declarative_part*]
    begin
        sequence_of_statements
    [**exception**
        { *exception_handler* }]
    end [*identifier*] ;

task_declaration ::= *task_specification*

task_specification ::=
    task [**type**] *identifier* [**is**
        { *entry_declaration* }
        { *representation_specification* }
    end [*identifier*]] ;

term ::= *factor* { *multiplying_operator factor* }

timed_entry_call ::=
    select
        entry_call [*sequence_of_statements*]
    or
        delay_statement [*sequence_of_statements*]
    end select;

type_conversion ::= *type_mark* (*expression*)

type_declaration ::=
    type *identifier* [*discriminant_part*] **is** *type_definition*;
  | *incomplete_type_declaration*

type_definition ::=
    enumeration_type_definition | *integer_type_definition*
    | *real_type_definition* | *array_type_definition*
    | *record_type_definition* | *access_type_definition*
    | *derived_type_definition* | *private_type_definition*

type_mark ::= *type_name* | *subtype_name*

unary_operator ::= + | − | **not**

use_clause ::= **use** *package_name* { , *package_name* };

variant_part ::=
    case *discriminant_name* **is**
        { **when** *choice* { | *choice* } =>
            component_list }
    end case;

with_clause ::= **with** *unit_name* { , *unit_name* };

Ada Reserved Words

The words in the following list are reserved by the language, as they have special meanings for the compiler. They cannot therefore be used as identifiers.

abort	declare	generic	of	select
accept	delay	goto	or	separate
access	delta		others	subtype
all	digits	if	out	
and	do	in		task
array		is	package	terminate
at			pragma	then
	else		private	type
	elsif	limited	procedure	
	end	loop		
begin	entry		raise	use
body	exception		range	
	exit	mod	record	when
			rem	while
		new	renames	with
case	for	not	return	
constant	function	null	reverse	xor

Index